Healing

WITH

HYPNO -

KINESTHETICS

Extraordinary
Mind Body Techniques for
Transformation!

By

PATRICIA ESLAVA VESSEY

INTEGRITY COACHING & TRAINING SYSTEMS

Dear Chieko,
May you always thrive
in the joy of movement
love
Patricia

ISBN NUMBER

978-1-7333666-0-1

LIBRARY OF CONGRESS NUMBR

Kindle ISBN: 978-1-7333666-1-8

Integrity Coaching & Training Systems
www.integritycoachingandtraining.com

HEALING WITH
HYPNO-KINESTHETICS:
*Extraordinary Mind Body
Techniques for Transformation!*
1st Edition, By Patricia Eslava Vessey
Patricia@integritycoachingandtraining.com

Cover image: Spiral Meanings

The Spiral is one of the oldest symbols. It symbolizes expansion, growth, evolution, connection, development of the mind, and continual motion and balance.

DISCLAIMER: This book educates you on ways to use self-coaching for personal development, business, and mind, body, and emotional wellbeing. Coaching, Mentoring, Consulting, Hypnosis, NLP, Mindfulness, and Hypno-Kinesthetics are stand-alone, help-care professions, and not therapy or licensed healing arts professions. These proud disciplines are wildly popular because of their profoundly positive results.

The author and publisher expressly disclaim responsibility for any adverse effects arising from the use or application of the information contained in this book and encourages you to seek services of competent helpers of all medical, health professionals if needed.

While all attempts have been made to verify information provided in this publication, the author assumes no responsibility for errors, omissions, or contrary interpretation of the subject matter herein. Any perceived slights of specific persons, peoples, or organizations are unintentional. Wherever possible and retrievable, credit has been given to contributors.

PERSONAL NOTE FROM PATRICIA:

I can still recall how I felt in my 7th-grade speech class, waiting for my turn to present. I trembled uncontrollably and wanted nothing more than to run away as fast as I could. I felt sheer panic as I stumbled to the front of the room. My eyes stared at the words on my paper, blurred because my hands were shaking so bad. My classmates were laughing at me; I was sure of it. My heart pounded so hard it nearly lifted the shirt off my chest. The next day I dropped out of that class and for years avoided speaking in groups. Every time I thought about that memory, I'd feel those same devastating feelings of failure. And I'd tell myself I could never be a speaker. It was too terrifying, and I wasn't good enough or smart enough anyway. That memory grew and festered inside me, making me feel inferior. It kept me from taking control, overcoming those negative beliefs, and it prevented me from healing, growing, and feeling confident.

Most people harbor hurtful memories that trigger bad feelings, impede personal growth, and stop them from discovering and actualizing their gifts, skills, and abilities. Some people have traumatic, painful, shameful, and harmful memories that keep them trapped. Those feelings actually live in your body. If left unresolved, over time, these feelings can wreak havoc on your physical, mental, emotional, and spiritual health and well-being.

I wrote this book for you, to help you be your best. And if you work with people, these techniques will help you to help them too. In this book, you will learn that you express your thoughts and feelings through the words you use, and through the movements you make. As you train your mind to give voice to your body in movement, you grow exponentially in joy, self-knowledge, and overall well-being. And, you will learn how to heal and transform your feelings and memories through movement.

It's time to take control of these deep feelings and change them into something you can use to create the future you've always wanted. This is more than just 'letting go of the past.' It's finally doing something with what you've been feeling and transforming it into something exciting and powerful you can actually use.

Most of the time, we are taught just to push aside negative feelings. Whatever happened in the past is in the past, but do we ever really forget? No! And the reason is that those memories and the feelings attached to them are now a part of our bodies on a cellular level. And, past feelings and memories are not going to be released or let go until you take action to change them.

The techniques and approaches in this book are supported by science. I have successfully used them with my clients in one-on-one sessions, workshops, and seminars. They are transformational tools you can use right away to help yourself and others. You may be surprised to see how easy it is to transform your past into what you've wanted all your life, whether that is peace, tranquility, more energy, or simply more confidence in what you're about to do for yourself.

My protocols incorporate techniques learned over thirty years in my work as a social worker, fitness trainer, coach, hypnotherapist, and Neuro Linguistic Programming (NLP) practitioner. These ideas took time to develop, to test, and to see what worked for others. Historically, talk therapy, hypnosis, and NLP focused upon the cognitive, emotional perceptions, and used physiology only as cues or triggers for cognitive processes.

My approach, which I call "HypnoKinesthetics," uses physiology, movement, and the kinesthetic system to provide healing, transformation, and positive change. It adds a mind-body approach with proven disciplines like behavioral medicine, biofeedback, mindfulness, hypnosis, coaching, movement, and NLP, so you easily access your limitless potentials.

This integrated approach helped me overcome limiting childhood beliefs to become a confident and successful person, leader, practitioner, and trainer. I also experienced for myself how it's possible to heal, and change hurtful memories, let go, and create a more captivating future. What used to hinder me in the past is no longer an issue for my future. I've succeeded, and so have my clients who put to practice these techniques.

I've seen on a daily basis how combined physical movement and mind mastery positively enhance life, improve moods, promote wellness, generate healthy habits, increase self-compassion, and build community. They also put to rest trauma and limiting habits. The results are astounding!

You may also benefit further by working with a professional hypnotherapist, coach, NLP practitioner, or psychotherapist to engage in more in-depth healing work. But first, let's get you started with the basics so you can see for yourself where this information will take you. You'll be surprised how you can start healing today.

My hope is that this book will be a personal resource and guide for happiness and positive changes in your life, and in the lives of those you serve. The techniques in this book will support you in your quest to release and heal the past, improve your life, and further your self-discovery. Use them and see for yourself!

Helping people heal from their past, cultivate positive relationships, and thrive in life, is my purpose in life and gives me the greatest joy.

All the best!

Patricia

Connect with Patricia at:

patricia@integritycoachingandtraining.com

www.integritycoachingandtraining.com

To study with Patricia call: 206-459-2898

Enjoy!

WHAT OTHERS SAY ABOUT
PATRICIA ESLAVA VESSEY'S HYPNO-KINESTHETICS

"It was the best experience that I've ever had. The whole process was so amazing. It's going to be a game changer." **-Donna Nellman, CHt**

"A refreshingly, unique way to problem-solve. It really impacted me."
-Anthony Peters, CHt

"I now know how to successfully add body language along with words and thoughts to help myself and others! Thank YOU! This is really beautiful." **-Kelli von Heydekampf, CHt**

"...An amazing experience... Take it in and experience it."
-De'Anna Nunez, CHt

"Fantastic! HypnoKinesthetics far surpassed what I was expecting. I highly recommend it." **-Mariana Matthews, CHt**

"I discovered that my body really knew things I didn't consciously know." -
Annette Mertens, CHt

"It's definitely a new process that I think is going to be up and coming and is very exciting." **-Caryn Bird, CHt**

"... fascinating...I immediately saw positive results...highly recommended." -
Jo Moon

I DEDICATE THIS BOOK

TO

Anyone who wants to embrace their self-worth, overcome obstacles and achieve peak performance at home, work, and play.

CONTENTS

INTRODUCTION ....- 15 -

1: HOW TO GET THE MOST FROM THIS BOOK ....- 17 -

2: WHAT IS HYPNOKINESTHETICS? ....- 19 -

3: HOW HYPNOKINESTHETICS CAN HELP YOU ....- 23 -

4: WHAT THE MIND-BODY RESEARCH SAYS ....- 25 -

5: THE STRESS & CELLULAR MEMORY CONNECTION ....- 31 -

6: WHAT IS KINESTHETICS? ....- 37 -

7: DANCE/MOVEMENT THERAPY, MUSIC & RHYTHM ....- 41 -

8: SOMATIC PSYCHOLOGY RESEARCH ....- 47 -

9: HOW EMOTIONS ARE STORED IN THE BODY ....- 49 -

10: MEMORY BEYOND THE BRAIN ....- 53 -

11: INSTITUTE OF HEARTMATH DNA RESEARCH ....- 57 -

12: YOU CAN CHANGE YOUR DESTINY ....- 59 -

13: SUMMARY & INTRODUCTION TO HYPNOKINESTHETICS
TECHNIQUES ....- 61 -

14: THE COMPONENTS OF HYPNOKINESTHETICS ....- 63 -

15: IMPORTANT TERMS & CONCEPTS ....- 69 -

16: USING HYPNOKINESTHETIC TECHNIQUES ....- 73 -

   1: HK FOR MORNING-EVENING RITUAL ....- 74 -

   2: HK FOR SUCCESS ....- 75 -

   3: HK FOR CONFIDENCE ....- 76 -

   4: HK FOR MOTIVATION ....- 77 -

   5: HK FOR TEAMS (Work, Corporate, & Team Building) ....- 78 -

   6: HK FOR HEALING ....- 79 -

   7: HK FOR STRESS ....- 81 -

   8: HK FOR PAIN RELIEF-CHRONIC ....- 82 -

   9: HK MOTIVATION TO LOSE WEIGHT (AVERSION) ....- 83 -

   10: HK - TRANSFORM RESISTANCE TO EXERCISE ....- 85 -

   11: HK - SLEEP: SLEEP SUIT ....- 87 -

   12: HK LEARNING FROM FUTURE SELF ....- 88 -

   13: HK - GETTING WHAT YOU NEED NOW! ....- 89 -

   14: HK BODY TALK ....- 90 -

15: HK FINDING THE INTENTION..*- 91 -*

16: KINESTHETIC TIMELINE REGRESSION ....*- 92 -*

17: HK GOALS FOR THE FUTURE...*- 93 -*

18: DESIRED BEHAVIOR - FINDING SOLUTION ....*- 94 -*

17: HYPNOKINESTHETICS FOR SPORTS.............................- 97 -

19: HK - SPORTS & PEAK PERFORMANCE (Excel at Sport-Stacked Anchors).....................*- 97 -*

20: HK - SPORTS & PERFORMANCE (Eliminate Pre-Game Anxiety).........................*- 99 -*

21: HK - SPORTS & PERFORMANCE (Zone-of-Success) ....*- 100 -*

18: HYPNOKINESTHETICS FOR KIDS...................................- 101 -

22: HK FOR KIDS: (Confidence - Healthy Self-Love) ....*- 101 -*

23: HK FOR KIDS: (Super Power For Thoughts & Feelings) ....*- 103 -*

24: HK FOR KIDS: (Calm, Centered & Relaxed in the Moment) ....*- 104 -*

25: HK FOR KIDS: (Stepping Stones for Learning) ....*- 105 -*

26: HK FOR KIDS: (Improving Performance) ....*- 106 -*

27: HK FOR KIDS: (Positive Walking Affirmations)..*- 107 -*

19: HYPNOKINESTHETICS FOR QUICK HELP ....- 109 -

28: HK - QUICK HELP (Feeling Stuck) ....*- 109 -*

29: HK - QUICK HELP (Creating Healing Metaphors) ....*- 111 -*

30: HK CHANGING STATES (What in Life Makes You Most Proud?) ....*- 112 -*

31: KINESTHETIC NLP CHANGE PATTERN ....*- 113 -*

32: HK UNIFYING PARTS...*- 114 -*

20: ADDITIONAL MOVEMENT BASED NLP TECHNIQUES...............- 117 -

BILATERAL STIMULATION...*- 117 -*

FASTER EMOTIONAL FREEDOM TECHNIQUE...*- 118 -*

DANCING SCORE PATTERN..*- 120 -*

ENERGY MEDICINE TOOL..*- 121 -*

HAVENING: (NLP for Dissolving Fear, Mental Blocks, & Hesitation)......................*- 123 -*

SPATIAL ANCHORING & SORTING ....*- 124 -*

NLP ANCHORING ....*- 125 -*

CIRCLE OF EXCELLENCE...*- 126 -*

SAD TO GLAD - CHAINING ANCHORS..*- 127 -*

POWER STANCE: (Change Physiology)..*- 128 -*

VISUAL SQUASH TECHNIQUE ....*- 129 -*

NLP MODELING ....*- 130 -*

KINESTHETIC SWISH...*- 131 -*

COLLAPSING ANCHORS ....*- 132 -*

HAVENING FOR SELF-IMAGE: (Weight Loss & Self-Image) ....*- 133 -*

21: HYPNOKINESTHETICS TRAINING & CERTIFICATION ....- 135 -

CONCLUSION ....- 139 -

ABOUT THE AUTHOR ....- 141 -

A: THE POWER OF YOUR CHAKRAS ....- 143 -

B: AFFIRMATIONS & VISUALIZATION ....- 147 -

C: COACHING CORE COMPETENCIES ....- 155 -

OTHER BOOKS ....- 159 -

NOTES ....- 161 -

INDEX ....- 169 -

FOREWORD

An old proverb says,
"Knowledge is only a rumor until it is in the muscle."

Throughout my career in NLP, I have tried to support certain ideas, such as the importance of conscious, unconscious connection and positive communication, the power of the somatic mind, and finally, the importance of finding patterns that connect by seeking multiple descriptions of the same human experiences. In my perception, these ideas and concepts that are detailed in this book promote health, but more importantly, they promote creativity, generativity, and the possibility of new horizons emerging for you personally, and also for your families, communities, and our precious world.

I was very blessed to spend time with Dr. Milton Erickson in the mid-seventies. I began to understand the power of the unconscious mind, which has been referred to in the third generation of NLP as the "somatic mind". It was obvious that the relationship between the cognitive mind and the unconscious mind is key for our individual growth. Without the integration of these two minds, the one that lives in the head and the one that lives in the heart, there is quite often conflict. When there is a balance between the heart and the mind, there is balance within every aspect of life.

This skilled offering, *Healing With HypnoKinesthetics* by Patricia Eslava Vessey, does just that. It opens us up to the world of the unconscious mind, AKA, the body and the knowledge that lives "under movement." It underscores the importance of taking charge of your patterns of mind and body. Patricia shares powerful ways you can use positive communication in every life experience to heal, thrive, and be happy. As you tap into the world of your unconscious self with body movement- AKA, "HypnoKinesthetics" -you enter a powerful portal for positive results.

Patricia reminds you of the importance of the alignment and integration of the "reasons of the reasons" and the "reasons of the heart. Her approach abates conflict and evokes wholistic wisdom. Patricia teaches you to use self-hypnosis, meditation, NLP, coaching, and more to bring more and more of your true self to the world.

In the words of the famous dancer Isadora Duncan, "If I could say it, I wouldn't have to dance it." Patricia is reminding us to do just that...dance it and heal.

By Judith Delozier, MA, NLP University.

__Judith DeLozier__ is an original co-developer of the field in NLP and has made fundamental contributions to the development of many core NLP models and processes including Somatic Syntax and the Dancing Score, as well as many others. She is co-author of the __Encyclopedia of NLP__ (with Robert Dilts), and numerous books and articles on NLP and international training on NLP and personal development.

INTRODUCTION

"... your body knows exactly what it is doing and always does the best thing it can do under the circumstances. Consequently, if you are overweight, you may reasonably assume that the extra fat itself is your body's best adjustment to the circumstances you are providing."
-Jill Johnson

This book focuses on HypnoKinesthetics, a type of Behavioral Medicine. HypnoKinesthetics embraces interdisciplinary practices and research that focuses on how your thoughts, feelings, and behavior affect success, health, and wellbeing. As you read through these topics and perhaps learn new terminology, you'll be given tools to improve your life and heal cellular memories that might be hindering your spiritual, physical, or mental progress. These are techniques and guides that you can use as soon as you read about them. They are proven to work, to heal, and help you overcome stumbling blocks in your life. What you have in your hands is a key to unleashing all possibility once you are able to heal the past. By healing cellular memories, you're ready to create the future you've always desired, dreamed about, and wanted.

Behavioral medicine techniques often include hypnosis, biofeedback, mindfulness, movement therapies, and relaxation training to tap into your unlimited potential to overcome disempowering thoughts, feelings, behaviors, and more.

HypnoKinesthetics is a therapeutic system of behavioral medicine that facilitates change, healing, and powerful life solutions by accessing and expressing information stored within the powerful mind-body relationship.

Kinesthetic movement is the most authentic representation of who you are at any given moment.

In this book, you'll learn how to:

1. Remove roadblocks to success.

2. Access, release, resolve, heal, and transform unhelpful memories and emotions through movement.

3. Build confidence, enhance resilience, and discover unconscious resources to achieve peak performance.

4. Enhance your intuition, awareness, understanding, and body wisdom through movement.

5. Gain a basic understanding and of basic Neuro-Linguistic Programming (NLP), Time Line Therapy, Hypnosis, Coaching, and HypnoKinesthetics.

6. Learn more about stress and cellular memory research, dance and movement therapy, music, rhythm, and somatic research.

7. Lead yourself and others through these kinesthetic change techniques in one-to-one or group settings.

Please Note: This book, including every technique described, is not a replacement for medical or psychiatric help. If you're under medical, psychiatric, or other care, please consult with your practitioner first before participating in these techniques. The information in this book is intended to augment and support all efforts to bring you the relief you're seeking. When choosing a practitioner to work with, always check credentials, specialized training, length of time as a practitioner and testimonials, and always trust your intuition (or gut) when making your selection.

1:
HOW TO GET THE MOST
FROM THIS BOOK

"The mind's first step to self-awareness
must be through the body."
- George Sheehan

This book can be a powerful resource for you. It has the potential to educate, heal, and enhance the quality of life for those who participate in the techniques contained within.

Use the tools and techniques found here to benefit yourself, but also to help other people in your life to find their solutions and learn to self-manage their emotions and behavior. They will help build confidence and resilience in yourself and those you serve. Imagine how good it will feel to be able to share an effective way to truly help others improve their lives and end their struggles.

The research in mind-body science in this book will give you a foundation and understanding of how to use it successfully to help others. You'll be able to guide them through challenges and into wellness solutions.

"The journey toward self-discovery is life's greatest adventure."
-Arianna Huffington

What's unique about these techniques is that they involve movement which can be fun, energizing, and engaging. Movement helps access the wisdom that is stored in every cell of your body.

Also included in this book are several opportunities to pause and participate in HypnoKinesthetics Activities. And, HypnoKinesthetics Cases are sprinkled throughout to demonstrate the use of these techniques.

2:
WHAT IS
HYPNOKINESTHETICS?

"Our bodies forget nothing. Every fear, every memory, every joy, every trauma you've ever experienced can be traced back in your body. Your body remembers the stories your brain has forgotten."
- Lonerwolf

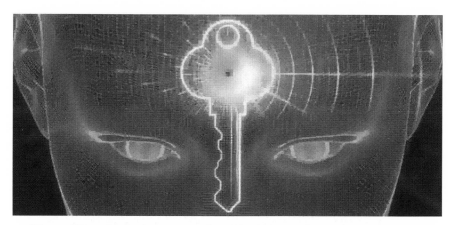

HypnoKinesthetics is a new and exciting personal empowerment system that combines NLP, coaching, hypnosis, and movement to help you heal the past, embrace the present and eagerly anticipate the future.

I created this system based on research from movement therapy, cellular memory theory, and mind-body science because it supports powerful change, healing, and transformation through physical movement. According to cellular memory theory, we store everything that's happened to us in our bodies. This means that every event we've experienced, including traumas, tragedies, and even triumphs and all their associated emotions have been memorialized, downloaded, and stored in the cellular tissues in our body. We know from research that if left unresolved, over time, this stored stress, trauma, and harmful memories can lead to physical, mental, and emotional problems like illness, injury, and disease.

And this can result in poor performance at work, school or sports; and create problems in relationships with self and others. The inability to feel happiness, joy and a sense of belonging and contribution can also be present. In other words, unresolved negative feelings can have a devastating effect on your entire life. Those memories are stored in your body, and with HypnoKinesthetics, we will use your body to heal and change them.

HypnoKinesthetics is a powerful and effective system that creates rapid and profound change. It can help you improve in all areas of your life by creating solutions to a multitude of life's challenges.

HypnoKinesthetics uses specific movement patterns and combinations that empower you to access, express, and heal unhelpful memories from the past that have been holding you hostage. Through movement, you will accentuate and enhance your positive memories to improve your skills and abilities today. And you will retrain the cellular memories in your body to create a compelling future and transform your life.

How is this done?

First, we choose a challenge in your life or an area of concern. Maybe you want more focus and confidence for a sports competition, job interview, to pass a test or to complete a big project, for example. We learn more about the event through coaching and questioning, find its location in the body, and then through specific movement patterns, the resolution is discovered and performed. Using HypnoKinesthetics, we essentially transform traditional talk therapy and other mental processes into solutions that are expressed through movement. Movement is defined as any physical movement such as gesturing, changing one's facial expression, lifting a finger, or touching your nose, for example. The movement could also include more active and energetic moves like jumping, for example. Ideally, the movement will be spontaneous and originate from the unconscious mind as an expression of the feeling state. These moves give you access to information stored within the powerful mind-body relationship, and it mobilizes the expression of deep resources.

HypnoKinesthetics can be used:

- In content-free sessions for those not wanting or able to access and verbalize problems

- To relieve stress, anxiety, fear, depression, procrastination, chronic health challenges, and other limiting beliefs and behaviors

- As an alternative way to heal and resolve problems while gaining inner knowledge

- To create clarity, focus, and follow through with goal setting and future planning

- By those who coach others and are tasked with getting people to change thoughts, feelings, and behaviors

- In one-to-one sessions with adults, teens, children, and the elderly
- By those struggling with performance issues like athletes, dancers, gymnasts, and other performers

Profound change can occur in just one session. However, several sessions will anchor and facilitate the manifestation of those changes and provide follow-up and accountability. HypnoKinesthetics includes a growing catalog of techniques and classes that allow you to experience powerful change work.

HypnoKinesthetics Benefits:

- Provides an innovative way to solve problems with movement
- Generates clarity not typically available
- Feels good to move
- Affects you in a profound way
- Changes the dynamics of the problem
- Improves clarity and healing and expand bigger each time you do it
- Cancels and clears the problem
- Identifies the cause of the problem and resources to solve it
- Creates more space and flexibility
- Adds fun and creativity
- Engages the mind body in a dynamic way
- Provides new and effective treatment options
- Helps to heal cellular memories, thus warding off illness, disease and improving health
- Improves kinesthetic awareness
- Causes a closer mind-body relationship
- Creates empowering physical rituals
- Anchors feelings
- Deliberately involves the body in healing the mind
- Provides a process for skill-building

- Replaces automatic behavior patterns

- Removes roadblocks

- Empowers your physical self

- Provides mastery of new skills

- Improves self-belief

3:
HOW HYPNOKINESTHETICS
CAN HELP YOU

"Re-programming your mind, body & spirit is like planting
a garden, if the soil isn't right nothing will grow."
- Nikki Rowe

HypnoKinesthetics can help.

HypnoKinesthetics can help with many problems because it is positive, intentionally healing, and the best part, life-changing and transformational.

I recently volunteered to teach confidence and self-management skills in several elementary schools. I was shocked, but not surprised, to hear from the mouths of these young children about the ongoing, overwhelming stress in their lives. The pressures that school-age children are experiencing range from forgetting to do their chores, homework, to passing tests.

Since 2014, the average stress levels in the U.S. have increased. According to studies, people are feeling increasing amounts of stress in their lives. And we as a race are feeling these stresses from a very young age.

When we face any stress in our lives, whether big or small, we can feel hopeless, helpless, and powerless to do anything about it. In an often turbulent world with much happening all the time, people become stressed, anxious, and worried. And their thoughts, feelings, and actions come from a place of fear and anxiety. Imagine instead your actions coming from a place of contentment, excitement, joy, and confidence. What would the world look like if we were positive and uplifting with one another? You might think it's too hard to change the way you think, handle stress, and act during difficult times, but this book will prove those doubtful thoughts wrong.

Our kids and teens suffer from high levels of stress as well and they're at risk of mental, emotional, and physical challenges according to studies. Psychologists worry about long-term health consequences if kids don't learn healthy ways to manage their stress at a young age.

Teachers and administrators need tips, tools, and techniques to help kids learn self-management skills so they can better cope with the stress and uncertainty in their lives. They need help facilitating inner growth and learning to improve the self-confidence of their students.

Coaches, therapist's, mental health workers, hypnotherapists, and others in the helping professions get stuck sometimes, not knowing what to do to help their clients.

Athletes and sports coaches need quick and effective ways to eliminate anxiety and build confidence. Coaches need tools to help their athletes consistently perform at their best, especially when the competition is fierce. Athletes have multiple stressors in their lives in addition to performing, and coaches need to help them with self-management.

Needless to say, everyone could use a little help learning to manage stress and in turn, teaching that to others. And, sometimes that help comes in the form of wisdom from others.

In my private Hypno-Coaching practice, I've worked with many disillusioned and downhearted leaders, workers, and team members who were stressed and anxious beyond measure. With little to no support from superiors, employees lack commitment, effectiveness, and personal empowerment in their roles. Leaders feel unsupported and unappreciated, and they lack the means and motivation to truly support their employees and build strong, healthy cohesive teams.

With growing health challenges, cost of living creases, and loneliness and isolation, our elder population also feels the adverse effects of chronic stress and anxiety. They need tools and techniques to change the way they think, feel, and act within their changing lifestyle. They, too, can benefit from the techniques in this book.

HypnoKinesthetics will help you find the remedies you're seeking, whether it's in the corporate world, medical field, athletics, with the elderly or children. I've written these techniques in an easy, accessible, step-by-step format designed to help you make those positive changes quicker and easier than ever before.

4:
WHAT THE MIND-BODY
RESEARCH SAYS

"The mind's first step to self-awareness must be through the body."
-George Sheehan

Have you ever heard an old song from your high-school days and suddenly felt emotional-maybe happy, sad or nostalgic? Maybe you can even remember tastes or smells associated with those memories. How do you feel when you think about seeing your best friend or beloved pet? Chances are you feel those good feelings somewhere in your body.

You store other emotions in your bodies as well. For example, stressful feelings may manifest as tension in the jaw, shoulders, or stomach. The fear of public speaking can be felt in the body as trembling, shortness of breath, and anxiety. Conversely, sensations in the body like pain, pressure, tightness, or even injury are most often related to an emotion you're feeling. Sometimes just thinking of having to do something you don't want to do will cause you to have an upset stomach and lose your appetite.

You have a carefully crafted and powerful mind-body relationship. Every event, experience, and emotion is memorialized and stored in your physical and mental bodies. At will, you can recall names, faces, places, feelings, and sometimes even scents and scenarios from long ago. Though you may forget many of these memories over time, they're permanently etched in our cellular memories, leaving physiological imprints.

Scientists believed for a long time, that memories were formed, processed, and sent to different destinations in the brain. Dr. Wilder Penfield, an American-Canadian neurosurgeon, was one of the first to accidentally discover this. In the 1950s, while working on an epilepsy cure, he electrically stimulated different areas of his patients' brains while they were under local anesthesia.

He discovered that when he stimulated various regions, they produced specific memories in the patient's life. This discovery led to the long-held belief that we store memories in the brain.

However, in 2004, there was a huge medical breakthrough in this area. During a research study at Southwestern University Medical Center in Dallas, scientists discovered that we store memories in the tissues, organs, and cells of the body, not just the brain. They believed these cellular memories were the true source of illness and disease. In one study, "surgeons removed every part of the brain and found the memories were always still there."

Dr. Eric Nestler, MD, of Harvard, said, "Scientists believe these cellular memories might mean the difference between a healthy life and death... Cancer can be the result of a bad cellular memory replacing a good one." He felt this research could provide one of the most powerful ways of curing illness. Imagine if all illness could be cured by dealing first with cellular memories? No longer would we need pills and invasive treatments to help deal with symptoms that could essentially be erased by instead focusing on cellular memories. In the same thought, imagine what you'll be able to feel once you start putting these techniques into action.

According to Dr. Bruce Lipton, formerly of Stanford University, our very cells hold the residue of fear and anger, which leads to 95% of all disease. The rest is caused by the exposing of a disease gene by stress somewhere in our cellular memory and ancestry.

Dr. John Sarno, NYU School of Medicine, agrees with Dr. Lipton and Dr. Nestler that adult chronic pain and illness originate from

destructive, unhealed cellular memories, and that healing cellular memory will take chronic pain and illness away. Dr. Sarno has conducted groundbreaking work in psychosomatic illnesses and the mind-body connection, specifically about back pain.

Dr. Andrew Weil, a holistic practitioner, agrees with Dr. Sarno that illness does not originate from a physical source. He says in his bestselling book, *Health and Healing*, that, "All illness is psychosomatic."

Think about it. What physical pains have you been experiencing? Are these recent pains, or issues that you have been dealing with for a long time? Do you have a physical problem that has been unresponsive and unfixed, no matter how hard you've tried or the countless doctors you've visited? Most people don't realize when they have an illness or pain in need of healing, is that they may also have contributing emotional pains and memories.

In his book, *The Sacred Life*, Davis Suzuki wrote, "Condensed molecules from breath exhaled from verbal expressions of anger, hatred, and jealousy contain toxins. These toxins, when accumulated over one hour, are enough to kill 80 guinea pigs!" Imagine the harm you are doing to your body when you stay in negative emotions or unprocessed emotional experience throughout your body.

The late Candace Pert, a Neuropharmacologist, author of *Molecules of Emotion*, NIH, Georgetown University Medical Center, made several ground-breaking discoveries and contributions in the area of cellular memories. Her research started a revolution in beliefs and a theory about how our thoughts and emotions are capable of creating wellness or disease in our bodies.

Our thoughts and emotions create either
wellness or disease in our bodies.

She says, "Everything is psychosomatic." The word "psycho" from the Greek language means breath, spirit, soul, mind. "Somatic" refers to the body, or "soma" in Greek, referring to the physical.

Dr. Pert also believed that our emotional memories, including all injuries and traumas, are stored in multiple locations in the tissues of the body, "not just, or even primarily, in the brain." Those thoughts and emotions "bubble up" from our bodies which we process and give meaning to according to our beliefs.

Dr. Pert said that the chemicals that are running our body and brain are the same. The mind and body are one system, and "neither can be treated separately without the other being directly affected." So, when treating illness in the physical body, healing must also take place in the mind.

She believed that the body is our subconscious mind, and we can't heal it by talk alone. We can, however, access our mind and our emotions through the physical body. So, we need to get in touch with our body through some mind-body work to access, heal, and release stuck emotions and traumas.

Joe Dispenza, New York Times bestselling author, researcher, and chiropractor says, when you recall a positive experience, "Your brain started firing those circuits created at the time of the event, the moment you recalled the experience." That experience and memory are wired together and produce in you a feeling of joy. And what most people don't know is that these positive memories can be used to help you heal and change.

The opposite is also true. A negative experience triggers a set of emotional, chemical, and physical responses that can have a very real impact on your life."

Despite what you might think about all of this research, these ideas are not new. Native cultures as far back as 6000 years ago connected mind, body, and spirit in their treatments and healing remedies. And, even Aristotle implied a connection between mood and health. He wrote, "Soul and body, I suggest, react sympathetically upon each other."

The Implications of this Research:

Scientist Howard Hall proved that we can train the way the cells function in the immune system using positive memories and suggestions through self-hypnosis, biofeedback, guided imagery, relaxation, and autogenic training. These interventions can help us actively influence our health and healing. We can work to retrain, rewire, and heal memories in our immune system and throughout our bodies.

We can actively influence our health and healing by retraining, rewiring, and healing memories in our immune system.

We can actively influence our health and healing by retraining, rewiring, and healing memories in our immune system.

Dr. Pert said, "My research has shown me that when emotions are expressed.... all systems are united and made whole. When emotions are repressed, denied, not allowed to be whatever they may be, our network pathways get blocked, stopping the flow of the vital feel-good unifying chemicals that run both our biology and our behavior." What this means is that healing, true healing, on a much deeper and profound level is available when we deal with the memories, the pain, the repressed feelings, and not just 'deal' with it, but heal it. This is much more than just 'letting it all out'. This is healing the way it should always be. HypnoKinesthetics is not positive thinking. It's taking healing through movement and creating new strengths, resources, and ultimately changing cellular memories.

HypnoKinesthetics Case 1.

Teri was passionate about a new business she wanted to start. But fear of failure kept her stuck, and she didn't act on her ideas. HK helped Terri find that fear in her body. She learned to express, heal, and resolve it through movement. Teri was free then to create that vision.

She found the inner resources of confidence and commitment, and she reinforced those resources in a movement pattern she used to support herself along the way. As a result of this work, Teri created her business and marketing materials and continues to pursue and embrace her success.

5:
THE STRESS & CELLULAR
MEMORY CONNECTION

"You have no need to travel anywhere. Journey within yourself, enter a mine of rubies and bathe in the splendour of your own light."
-Rumi

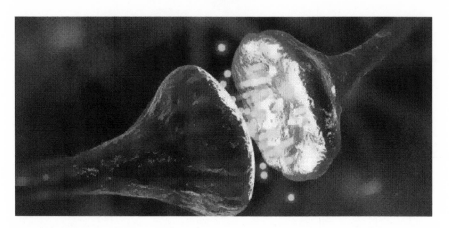

What is Cellular Memory?

In 2009, Harvard Medical School defined cellular memories as

"a sustained cellular response to a transient stimulus."

When a specific stimulus triggers a cell, it will consistently respond in a particular way, every time. In short, cellular memories are specific memories that are stored in the cells in your body. Every time you recall those memories, you will feel the same way each time you remember that memory. And this applies to both positive and negative cellular memories, which ultimately impact our health and wellbeing.

Your cellular memories can cause unhealthy, unwanted and negative symptoms in your lives.

Your cellular memories can cause unhealthy, unwanted and harmful symptoms in your lives, and here's how.

Every thought you have is either creating new neural connections in your brain or strengthening current ones. So, your thoughts are influencing every one of your seven octillions (7 with 27 zeros after it) atoms.

For example, each time you allow yourself to get mad when someone cuts you off in traffic, you're strengthening those neural connections in your brain. And over time, this makes your response automatic, and many times, unconscious. These neural networks are your cellular memory.

So, if you grew up with unhealed stress, drama, trauma, and anger, your life today may be filled with the same emotions that continue to resurface. Your brain uses cellular memories to determine how to respond to everything in life. That's why you may keep making the same unhealthy and unsafe choices, even though consciously you may know better. And if left unhealed and unresolved, those cellular memories can lead to your unhappiness, ill health, failure, and devastation.

The theory of cellular memories states that memories, and personality traits, are not only stored in the brain but also stored in the various organs in the body, such as the heart. It's is not hard to believe this since heartache, passion, and love are all associated with the heart. One fascinating way to understand cellular memory is by studying organ transplants.

Organ Transplants and Cellular Memories:

There are many extraordinary stories about transplant recipients acquiring traits from their donors. One famous and fascinating story is about Claire Sylvia, a health-conscious professional dancer, choreographer, and recipient of a heart and lung transplant. After her transplant, she began acting differently and having strange dreams. She developed a craving for beer, burgers, and chicken nuggets, which she didn't eat before. Claire also started wearing different colors and liking different music. Later, she discovered that these preferences were those of her 18-year-old donor. These experiences impacted her so much that she wrote about them in her book, *A Change of Heart.*

Another extreme case was an 8-year-old girl who received a 10-year-old girls' heart. After surgery, she began to have nightmares of a man trying to kill her. Her dreams were so vivid that her parents sent her to a psychiatrist. The girl described the murderer in such detail that they contacted the police. And it was later discovered that the little girl's donor had been murdered. The details of the murderer allowed the police to find the killer and convict him of murder.

In another case, an Australian girl's blood type was changed nine months after she received a liver transplant. This resulted in the girl acquiring her donor's immune system too, due to the stem cells of her new liver transferring over to her bone marrow. It was as if she had a bone marrow transplant.

Other documented cases have been baffling and sometimes extreme. A 47-year-old man received a heart from a 17-year-old African American boy and violinist. The man suddenly picked up an intense fondness for classical music. The donor, a 17-year-old boy, was killed in a drive-by shooting, still clutching his violin case in his hands.

Cellular memories stored throughout your body, and they are stamped with your unique, lifetime of experiences. These transplant stories show us that cellular memories are permanently And they can be transferred to the recipient's and even change their personality.

This cellular memory theory applies to all of us without exception. Your cells are imprinted with your history and every experience you've had until now. And, those experiences dictate your thoughts, beliefs, feelings, and behavior.

You cannot change what's happened to you, but those memories of trauma, abuse, neglect, disappointment, unhappiness, and failure can be healed and changed.

It's incredible to imagine that everything that makes you can be transferred into another person. The same reality can be applied to what needs to be healed inside of you to allow you to truly be at peace, to let go of painful memories, and discover new possibilities in life.

With HypnoKinesthetics, hypnotherapy, NLP, coaching, and other alternative modalities, you can change those cellular memories while designing and immersing yourself in a thriving, healthy, and happy future.

Stress and Cellular Memories:

When I was a social worker and supervisor-manager in a child-protective, government agency, I was in and out of the doctor's office and on antibiotics nearly every other month for 30 years. Now that I'm retired from that job, I hardly ever see the doctor!

The daily stress of removing kids from abusive homes, court litigations, politics, and ever-changing rules in state government took its toll on my emotional and physical body. When I removed that stress associated with those memories from my life, I was finally able to heal my mind and body for the first time during my career.

According to The American Institute of Stress, 75-90 percent of all doctor visits are related to stress. Workplace stress costs $125 - $190 billion a year, according to a study in 2015. This study looked at "The Relationship Between Workplace Stressors and Mortality and Health Costs in the United States." It isn't too hard to believe when everyone faces stress each day. But this stress is not just harmful to our minds, but also our bodies.

Dr. Doris Rapp, a pediatric allergist, and author of the best-selling book Is This Your Child, talks about how we accumulate stress in our body. She describes a cellular memory principle called the "barrel effect." Imagine a big barrel inside your body that contains all your stress. We can live with daily stress as long as that barrel is not full. But once it's full, any additional stress can create a crisis.

For example, today, your stress barrel maybe half full and you eat shellfish and feel fine. Several days later, your stress barrel may be overflowing, and eating shellfish causes an allergic reaction.

According to Dr. Rapp's research, stress is the deciding factor that causes you to respond unfavorably. You can see this in children who are regularly exposed to allergens, viruses, and bacteria but aren't always affected. The internal source of stress can affect you mentally and emotionally as well causing overreactions, conflicts, and trauma.

HypnoKinesthetics Case 2.

12-year-old Sally seemed to always be anxious and stressed about schoolwork and expectations at home. Her parents and teachers were concerned. As an infant, Sally had health problems which required numerous medical appointments. She became anxious, fearful and dreaded each appointment. This anxiety, stress and pressure had become a permanent part of Sally's personality. With HypnoKinesthetics, Sally learned to access those anxious feelings and memories in her body. She allowed them to heal through movement. And she replaced them with more helpful thoughts and feelings.

Ancestral Memories:

You have a fear based, automatic, and cellular response designed to keep you safe. And, you may have inherited it from your ancestors. Ancestral stress can also affect you.

The trauma, anxiety, depression, addictions, health issues, etc., experienced by your ancestors can be passed down to you in cellular memories like DNA.

This stress, due to cellular memories, which may be affecting you so strongly may NOT even be *yours*. The source of every mental, emotional, spiritual, and physical problem can be linked to your cellular memories, according to research by many of these experts.

In spite of this research, unfortunately, traditional medicine still believes that using the mind to understand the body is "unscientific." They believe the mind affecting the body is "psychosomatic" and therefore somehow not relevant.

PAUSE NOW AND TRY THIS ACTIVITY.

Close your eyes, think about, and remember a happy time in your life. Maybe you were having a good time or doing something really fun, and you were happy. As you remember this happy time, notice what images come to mind. Maybe you can remember everything you saw during that time. Perhaps you remember what sounds you heard during this memory. Maybe there are sounds from nature or people, or you remember what you were saying to yourself. Remember how you felt during this happy time. What are these feelings? How would you describe these feelings? What is the sensation? Where do you feel these feelings in your body?

Now, allow these good feelings to grow and spread throughout your entire body. Feel these happy, good feelings grow and spread all the way up to the tip of the longest hair on your head and all the way down and through the soles of your feet. Every bone, muscle, tendon, ligament, cell, and fiber of your body is now saturated with these good feelings. Then intensify these feelings, double and triple and quadruple these good feelings making them stronger and stronger and stronger.

Now, if your body were to express these good feelings in a movement or gesture of some kind, what would that be? Allow your body to manifest these good feelings in a movement or gesture now. Repeat that movement or gesture 3-5 times. How does it feel to express that emotion through movement? Repeat that movement 3-5 times or more, and feel the feelings becoming stronger as you add this movement to your muscle memory. When you are done, you can write down everything you felt, thought of, and the action associated with that memory.

6:
WHAT IS
KINESTHETICS?

"Words represent your intellect. The sound, gesture
and movement represent your feelings."
- Patricia Fripp

Kinesthetics is the study of body motion and the perception
(both conscious and unconscious) of one's body motions.

Kinesthetics are involuntary, unconsciously produced movements of the body in response to a thought, feeling, or idea. It is the study of body motion and the perception (both conscious and unconscious) of one's body motions. Kinesthetic awareness means how you sense your body. It's what gives you a sense of presence and of being alive. The word "kinesthetic" comes from Greek kinein "to move" and aisthesis "sensation." So, it means "feeling of movement."

Kinesthetics helps you understand ideas more quickly by feeling. Trauma, lack of body awareness, or abuse or injury can cause your kinesthetic awareness to become distorted.

According to Meir Schneider, founder of the School for Self-Healing in San Francisco, many people have poor kinesthetic awareness because "We have been numbing ourselves." He goes on to say that, "A major cause of poor kinesthetic awareness is fear. We are afraid to feel. We don't tune in to what the body really wants because we are afraid of what we might find. However, the sense of who you are comes largely from the body, from the kinesthetic sense."

Kinesthetic awareness is fundamentally essential to physical well-being and human potential, according to Alexander, Moshe Feldenkrais, Mabel Todd, and Charlotte Selver, leaders in the field of somatic education. The depth of its importance remains mostly unrecognized.

Movement can be an exploratory way to uncover hidden and repressed information while accessing solutions and healing.

It's a means of communicating with your unconscious mind. It's a way to communicate nonverbally.

Accessing information through movement is powerful for many reasons. Since the unconscious mind functions on a metaphorical level, dealing with imagery and imagination rather than logic (systems that use the body and emotions rather than our verbal skills), they're highly effective in reaching that part of the mind.

Movement communicates with the unconscious, pre-verbal parts of the mind.

HypnoKinesthetics can be highly effective because many problems originate in the pre-verbal part of the mind. Your body movements are in response the signals sent to it from the mind. This happens even when you think it doesn't.

HypnoKinesthetics externalizes the internal, unearthing what's inside and bringing it out through movement.

If the mind-body is injured by trauma, anxiety or depression, it can be healed by moving the body and learning new ways to release and repair.

HypnoKinesthetics collapses the distance between the mind and body, as well as increases your awareness of how buried feelings impact the relationship with self and others.

"Kinesthetic relates to learning through feeling such as a sense of body position, muscle movement and weight as felt through nerve endings."

An example of kinesthetics is working out in an exercise class, or learning to ride a bike by getting on the bike and riding, not just hearing about how to do it.

You construct your mental maps of the world through representational systems. In NLP, they're known as sensory channels, visual, auditory, kinesthetic gustatory and olfactory. Feeling and or movement uses the kinesthetic representation system. The ability to access these channels and this information is within each of us. However, most of us have a preferred, or most commonly used channel.

The kinesthetic learning system teaches body awareness, gives a sense of personal power, strength, and resilience (perhaps not generated from other sources or life events). It can also change belief systems and problem-solving abilities. You are indeed a very powerful person. Isn't it exciting to be now learning just how much control you really do have over yourself and your destiny? You are not hopeless, helpless, or alone. You, and you alone, have everything you'll ever need to heal and succeed.

F.M. Alexander, the developer of The Alexander Technique, talks about kinesthetic dysfunction, an inability to sense your body accurately. He wrote, "There can be no doubt that man on the subconscious plane now relies too much on a debauched sense of feeling or sense-appreciation for the guidance of his psychophysical mechanism, and that he is gradually becoming more and more overbalanced emotionally, with very harmful and far-reaching results."

According to this theory, for many, body awareness is missing, which means you cannot tell if you're tense or relaxed. This tension can come from psychological trauma, anxiety, or distress, as well as physical injury. Because you can't feel it, it goes unnoticed. This lack of awareness makes it challenging to access remedies that can support and heal the body. And, it can lead to injury, ailments, and long-term pain over time.

You can increase your kinesthetic awareness and help those you serve to improve their body awareness in many ways. Getting them to touch, tense, and relax muscles will raise body awareness. Doing this helps to access different sensory stimuli creating new neural connections, and it rekindles the kinesthetic sense. Increasing your client's kinesthetic awareness and movement is an essential aspect of healing and change work.

Practicing mindfulness, engaging in bodywork, walks, Tai Chi, Pilates, weight training, dance, yoga, and other forms of exercise will improve your kinesthetic awareness too. And your presence and kinesthetic expertise will affect the success of your clients.

HypnoKinesthetics Case 3.

Joy was struggling to losing weight. She was pre-diabetic, and desperately trying to create an exercise habit because she remembered in earlier years, how good she felt when exercising regularly. She also wanted to be consistently making good food choices. Joy realized through HK that this problem started when she became a parent and stopped doing things for herself.

Instead, she placed everyone's needs before her own. And in the process, she became overweight and developed unhealthy habits. What she wanted was to exercise consistently because it felt good, it would give her energy, and it would improve her health. HK allowed her to discover the origin of the problem, express, and find a solution through movement. She was then able to find the confidence and motivation to change.

7:
DANCE/MOVEMENT THERAPY, MUSIC & RHYTHM

"I see dance being used as communication between body and soul, to express what is too deep to find for words."
- Ruth St. Denis

Dance/Movement Therapy (DMT) (defined by the American Dance Therapy Association (ADTA)) is the psychotherapeutic use of movement to promote emotional, social, cognitive, and physical integration of the individual to improve their health and well-being.

It is a non-verbal movement technique used to communicate and express ones' spirit and emotions.

We are always engaged in motion. Rhythmical motility, the ability to move spontaneously, or "dancing," is a means of direct expression. It is often more precise and direct than verbalization.

This inner dance is often an unconscious, spontaneous reaction to how we are feeling and how we view our immediate environment.

All movement, including dance, is a representation of your unconscious thoughts, feelings, and emotions. It is an authentic expression of who you are.

Dance/Movement Therapy (DMT):

As one of the oldest forms of human expression, dance is used throughout many cultures for celebration, religious and social expression, meditation, healing, and communication.

At the beginning of the 20th Century, "modern dance" evolved to allow internal feelings to express what is impossible to convey with words. Pioneers such as Isadora Duncan, Rudolf of Laban, and Mary Wigman provided the innovation and foundation for dance therapy.

In 1942, a dancer named Marian Chace is considered the principal founder of what is now considered dance therapy. She is accredited with leading the movement of dance in the medical community. Her work gained recognition by doctors after her students reported feelings of improved well-being. Doctors and psychiatrists began sending patients to her dance classes. In 1966, Marian became the first president of the American Dance Therapy Association, an organization which she and several other DMT pioneers founded.

Dance/Movement Therapy, a form of psychotherapy, is a non-verbal movement technique used to communicate and express ones' spirit and emotions.

The purpose of DMT is to help you gain more self-awareness while improving your sense of self. It also allows a more significant connection with the conscious and unconscious parts of your personality.

Dance is not just therapeutic for patients. Professional dancers, as seen on TV dance shows like *World of Dance, Dancing with the Stars, and So You Think You Can Dance*, talk about the mental, emotional, and physical benefits of dance. They talk about how it helped them heal and manage challenging, traumatic, and uncertain times.

Movement is a means to express emotions and heal. Dance, a sometimes-structured form of movement, allows the expression of feelings and emotions through nonverbal techniques. It allows for creative expression and provides a sense of coping and freedom.

According to research, it's a useful form of support and intervention for abused children, too. The effects of dance intervention are also found to be therapeutic for psychiatric patients and those who are emotionally challenged as well.

Movement is the medium of dance therapy just as words are the medium of oral therapy.

Your body is the most fundamental tool you have for living in the world and building your future. Your thoughts manifest through your body in words, voice tone, facial expression, body posture, and movement.

> **"If you listen to music, dance daily, and meditate, you have the best medicine for your mind, body, and soul."**
> **- Lailah Gifty Akita**

With HypnoKinesthetics, you use this unconscious and precise movement in a therapeutic approach to access unhelpful memories, express challenges, and find their resolutions. This can occur through spontaneous movement, or it may be a connection of moves.

The Power of Movement, Music, and Rhythm:

These three are an integral part of your everyday life. You connect time, places, and meaningful memories with the emotions they evoke; your attitudes and moods are influenced and even guided by them. They access parts of the nervous system that are not typically available to you, and they activate more intuitive right brain types of thinking. They promote wellness and help with stress management and stimulate endorphins and oxytocin while energizing, helping with mood, motivation, endurance, and physical performance.

Rhythm guides your life. Your heartbeat keeps a unique and particular pace. The way your lungs breath in and out is stamped with your specific pattern of movement. And your internal systems move to a rhythm unique to you.

Your brain's pleasure center releases the neurotransmitter, dopamine, which makes you feel happy when you hear enjoyable music. Music can also help to release immunity-boosting antibodies and cells that protect you against bacteria and other invaders. And it is effective in helping to treat a variety of conditions ranging from premature birth to depression to Parkinson's disease.

Using music with HypnoKinesthetics can help to deepen the experience, anchor the changes, and create new positive cellular memories.

Music can also help with meditation, self-healing, self-hypnosis, sleep, and provide a calming sense of well-being.

As you think about movement, music, and rhythm, how can you implement these powerful resources in your life today? It could be listening to one of your favorite songs, especially from your childhood, and feeling that joy and happiness. Perhaps you'll play it and move to the rhythm, dancing here and there throughout the house. This is a little thing that could prove to be useful in helping to heal underlying cellular memories in your body.

Movement Research in Psychotherapy:

An essential goal in psychotherapy is teaching patients and clients to regulate their emotions by enhancing or decreasing certain feelings. Doing so can both improve and eradicate symptoms in a variety of mental health disorders.

The typical therapeutic techniques for emotional regulation focus mostly on cognitive strategies such as reappraisal, distancing, distraction, or behavioral strategies such as exposure for desensitization or response modulation. However, one of the most readily available, but underused strategy is using body movement to regulate emotion.

There have been differing beliefs among scientists about the origins of emotions and bodily responses. However, Antonio Damasio, a neuroscientist, reformulated a theory which states that emotions are generated in the body and sent to the brain. This concept implies that through deliberate control of motor behavior (movement), we could adjust our emotions and affect our feelings. This approach is compatible with the latest neurophysiological findings, and it's consistent with NLP theory. And since we are always in some form of movement or posture, through movement we can continuously alter and regulate our emotional state through our movement patterns.

Dance psychotherapists use this concept as they help patients evoke, enhance, and regulate specific emotions by directing them to move in certain ways.

...through deliberate control of motor behavior (movement), one could adjust his emotions and affect his feelings.

Being able to use this concept is vital for talk therapists as well. It's an alternative way within which to support healing, improvement and change in patients/clients.

Using movement to enhance and regulate feelings can be a useful skill for the therapist to cultivate for themselves as well.

This concept is sometimes used in other therapeutic settings where patients are encouraged to engage in different movement patterns to evoke emotions. This may include directing them to smile to elevate and enhance happiness, even when smiling is artificial.

Body movement, such as specific breathing patterns and muscle relaxation are also techniques that help regulate emotional states.

Exercise is scientifically proven to be effective in regulating emotions and is regularly recommended as an alternative to medication to reduce depression and anxiety.

Using this kind of therapy requires years of specialized training. HypnoKinesthetics can help clients regulate emotions, and it provides additional benefits and options as well. The exciting thing about learning these concepts is discovering the movement patterns your body comes up with that helps you produce the feelings you want to have. As you continue to learn how important it is to use movement to heal cellular memories, I hope you will be inspired. And maybe you'll begin to add additional types of movement to your life.

In HypnoKinesthetics, emotional regulation and change work originate from using a simple framework within which clients/patients discover, express, and resolve problems using their inner resources. That's right. You are already capable of being successful at using HK. Rather than the practitioner directing self-discovery and change, clients discover and manifest their solutions and healing. This model is empowering as well as confidence and independence building. HypnoKinesthetics techniques can be a quick, easy, and powerful way to help clients/patients achieve the goals they want while building self-reliance, self-discovery, and confidence.

Neuroscientists Jean Decety and Julie Grèzes discovered that when we visualize ourselves being confident or doing something, our brain acts as if it's happening. This simulated event causes a sensory experience that can include physiological changes in heart rate, respiration, and even emotion. Practicing visualization can be instrumental in building new skills, goal achievement, and emotion management. Visualization (Appendix B) can provide tremendous help to people who have a disability or who have limited motor capabilities.

HypnoKinesthetics Case 4.

Debby had trouble sleeping and suffered from insomnia. She would lay awake and try to solve problems at work and in her personal life. Then she would get anxious about not being able to sleep, which caused many sleepless evenings. We talked about taking time during the day to practice mindfulness, deep breathing, and to make time for herself.

We discussed preparing for sleep, winding down, powering off electronics, etc. Through the use of HK Morning and Evening Rituals, Debby was able to clear worries from the day and go to sleep with gratitude and good thoughts. The morning ritual helped her set the tone for the day and how she wanted to "be" in it. She began sleeping better and feeling calmer in her life.

8:
SOMATIC
PSYCHOLOGY RESEARCH

"Your thoughts, feelings and memories, live in your physical self so by utilizing physical expression and body wisdom, you evoke the life you want. So let's allow your body full expression and be your best."
- Shelley Stockwell-Nicholas

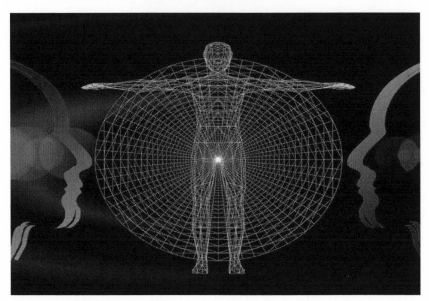

The word somatic comes from the Greek word "soma," which means body. Somatic therapy focuses on the relationship between the mind and body in regard to the psychological past. According to theory, stress is caused by triggering cellular memories of past traumas. When a stressor becomes unbearable, it overloads your autonomic nervous system (ANS), and you get stuck in a traumatic energy state. This trauma gets stored in the muscles, fascia, tissues, and organs of your body. Your brain blocks the experience often becoming fragmented.

That's the scientific way that stress becomes embedded in the body and in turn, causes physical symptoms. Stress can be considered a disease. We can understand the causes and learn the techniques that help us get rid of it. But when stress becomes unbearable, the body will respond in kind. Basically put, since we all experience stress, we need to get rid of that stress before it takes a long-term toll on our bodies.

Unless you find a way to release traumatic cellular memory, you carry around these negative imprints and emotions in your body throughout life. And, they can be triggered by a multitude of positive and negative stimuli such as fear-inducing events, people, sights, sounds, and even through bodywork, meditation, or yoga. With HypnoKinesthetics, we can find where memories are stored and through movement, release and transform them to facilitate more helpful, healthy, and empowering states, and neutralize those other memories.

HypnoKinesthetics Case 5.

Mark had been playing golf for eight years. After working with a pro, he learned everything needed to be skilled and play good golf. However, there was one point in his swing where Mark consistently froze, and that prevented him from a successful swing even though he possessed the skill to do it. During our work, he discovered that sticking point represented a feeling of inadequacy from childhood related to his older brothers' success in sports. With HK, he found the source of that sticking point in his body, expressed, healed, and resolved it, while giving himself the inner resources he needed to be successful in golf. Mark went on to perfect his swing.

9:
HOW EMOTIONS ARE
STORED IN THE BODY

"The body is a self-healing organism, so it's really about clearing things out of the way so the body can heal itself."
-Barbara Brennan

We know that your mind carries your emotional stress, but your body does, too. Unresolved stressful emotions and painful memories can hurt your body. And, the physical clues you experience could be illuminating signs of those emotional memories.

Western-trained doctors and neuroscientists often report that human emotions and memory are stored in the amygdala or limbic system. However, your body holds onto your past too.

PAUSE NOW AND TRY THIS ACTIVITY.

Remember a stressful time in your life. Now, go inside yourself and notice where you feel that stressful thought in your body. Where do you feel those stressful feelings? Where do they live in your body, and what is the sensation? If that stressful feeling had a color, what would it look like? If there was a sound associated with that feeling, what would it sound like? If there was a taste or smell associated with those feelings, what would it be? If you expressed that feeling in a movement or gesture, what would that movement or gesture be? Perform that movement now. How does it feel to express that feeling through movement? If you were to know, what needs to happen inside you for that feeling to be neutralized or transformed into something more helpful, what would that be? See, sense, feel, and imagine what would neutralize or transform that feeling. When you know what that is, focus on it, intensify it, and let it grow stronger and stronger.

Now allow this transforming feeling to express itself in a movement. Repeat it 3-5 times. Then, express the stress movement, then the transforming movement. Go back and forth. Now, remember those happy feelings from before and express that movement or gesture. Repeat until you feel a positive shift. Notice how you feel. Repeat that movement 3-5 times or more, and feel the feelings becoming stronger as you add this movement to your muscle memory. When you have finished, you can write down everything you felt, thought of, and the movement associated with that memory. You can create a journal of all sorts of happy memories and movements and return to them whenever you need them.

How does our body experience emotions?

There was an interesting study in 2013 about how we experience emotions in the body. Both European and Asian participants were asked to identify where they actively felt various emotions on a body map. The emotions, both complex and basic, ranged from love to shame.

It was discovered that many participants felt anger and pride in the head, neck, and shoulders. They felt love and happiness throughout almost their entire body, especially the heart. Anxiety and fear are felt in their chest, which is consistent with most of the clients I've seen in my practice. And, depression was felt in most of the body, especially the limbs. The sensation of these feelings is felt almost instantly. For example, a negative emotion triggers tension in the jaw and around the eyes and mouth.

Did you know that repeated or ongoing negative sensations can change the body? According to neurophysiologists, repeated stress can shorten the neck and shoulder muscles. Depression can cause a tight brow, and an increased mental workload can result in muscle tension in the cervical and shoulders. It is no wonder that most over the counter pain pills now advertise for daily pain relief instead of occasional use.

These body changes can lead to chronic pain, discomfort, and limited mobility. One theory is that muscle tension decreases blood flow, leading to lower oxygen delivery, lactic acid buildup, and the accumulation of toxic metabolites. Shortening of the muscle fibers can also activate pain receptors. Lack of movement can further reduce blood flow and oxygenation.

You can release stored negative emotions in a variety of ways. Seek the help of a professional to help you change your thoughts, learn mental training techniques, or address the root cause. Then, make lifestyle changes and heal from your past traumas. You can actively participate in physical activities such as yoga, Tai Chi, Pilates, HypnoKinesthetics, running, weight training, dance, etc. to help release tension in your body.

HypnoKinesthetics Case 6.

Anne suffered from acute pain in her low back. Working in her current job, which was extremely stressful, caused the pain, and aggravated it. She had tried numerous treatments, including medication, to no avail. HK allowed Anne to identify the reason for the pain through movement while finding the resources that helped her heal and release it.

10:
MEMORY BEYOND
THE BRAIN

"When the mind, body, and spirit work together,
I believe anything is possible."
- Criss Angel

There is ample scientific evidence proving memory storage in locations other than the brain.

Additional examples of the body containing exceptional memory capabilities are:

1. Your memory T-cells enhance the immune system's response by maintaining information about previous attacks by specific foreign antigens. Because of this memory, your body can initiate a protective response.

2. The ability of world-class athletes, musicians, actors, and other performers, to perform optimally even under extreme pressure is due mostly to muscle memory.

3. Genetic research has demonstrated that the matrix composing our body's cells (DNA) possess a complex information storage system.

When considering the vastness of your body's intelligence, it's no wonder that every part of your body is capable of holding memories.

Healing Cellular Memories:

According to scholars, there's no true healing without healing the cellular memories - physically or non-physically!

Your physiology, your thoughts, beliefs, emotions, and your behavior are all manifestations of your cellular memories and the beliefs that come from them.

Willpower, traditional therapy, and even conscious desensitization are NOT very effective because they don't get to the source of the real problem.

Nor do these methods provide lasting cellular healing. Instead, often they program your unconscious to repress those memories and disconnect your emotional responses from them. This is called coping, not cellular healing, and it often causes people to feel numb, stressed, and unable to manage effectively. Even if you don't remember those memories actively, they may still be influencing your thoughts, feelings, and actions and thus are causing problems.

Repression plus coping does not help to heal cellular memories.

I've worked with many trauma victims who thought they had healed a past traumatic event, only to discover more healing was necessary. Eventually, we would end up working on that event because it hadn't been resolved before, merely repressed or hidden. Sometimes even traditional therapy can go on for years and fail to bring about real healing growth and change.

For true healing, you need to locate and heal the source, which is the original cellular memory that's triggering this reaction. Doing this will stop that response signal that is turning off your immune system and negatively impacting your body.

For that to work, you need powerful tools like HypnoKinesthetics, hypnosis, and NLP, which are capable of helping to heal and reprogram cellular memories with more than just willpower or words.

Even though you think of memories as being in your past, they are very much in *your present* to the unconscious mind.

You can still access them and change the way they affect you in the present.

Memories are sometimes unreliable or they contain misinformation, so we're often unable to know the exact details. However, you do remember the feelings and beliefs associated with a past painful event, which is even more important than the details. And those feelings and memories can be changed. For example, you may not recall the exact details of an unpleasant interaction with someone, but you'll remember how badly they made you feel which you'll dwell on most. And, even though it may be painful, unhealthy and illogical, you may recreate these scenarios in your life because they are familiar and they are anchored in your body. But, to overcome that, you must find a way to heal from that first bad situation.

With hypnosis, NLP, and HypnoKinesthetics, you can heal and change the emotional effects of those memories.

HypnoKinesthetics Case 7.

John had recovered from surgery for brain cancer over 6 years ago, but struggled cognitively to accomplish tasks, set goals, socialize, and have fun. In hypnosis, it was discovered by the unconscious mind, that there were disconnected wires in John's brain. So, through guidance and HK, John physically repaired the connections. This caused a huge change in him. From this point on John went on to take classes, develop and achieve goals, and spend more time having fun.

What this means is that harmful and destructive thoughts and emotions like anger, hatred, bitterness, and others, are ultimately translated by the brain as stress.

And this stress changes the expression of our very own DNA.

Your body manifests stress like anger, anxiety, tension, impatience, nervousness, and other responses that, if left unresolved overtime, have destructive consequences in your body. That's your mind and body's response to toxic thinking. Even a little stress from toxic thinking has far-reaching consequences for your mental and physical health according to research.

You cannot always control the events or circumstances of your life, but you can learn to have 100% control over the way you think, feel, and respond.

11:
INSTITUTE OF HEARTMATH
DNA RESEARCH

"The body is wise; the confusion is from the mind."
- Aniekee Tochukwu

An experiment conducted by the Institute of HeartMath shows that our thoughts and feelings can change the shape and reaction of our DNA. When the researchers felt love, gratitude, and appreciation, the DNA responded by unwinding, becoming longer, and relaxing.

When they felt stress, anger, fear, or frustration, the DNA responded by tightening, becoming shorter, and switching off many of the DNA codes. The researchers discovered later with HIV patients that negative thoughts, feelings, and emotions are reversible with positive feelings of love, joy, appreciation, and gratitude. They also found that HIV positive patients with these positive thoughts and feelings had 300,000 times the resistance!

That's why discovering and learning how to change your thoughts and emotions to create new positive cellular memories will improve your life. This can mean the difference between a healthy mind and body- or a sick one.

According to research, 75-98% of mental and physical illnesses come from our thoughts! Just imagine how better you'll feel, the things you'll be able to accomplish, when you heal on a cellular level. You'll be able to achieve any goal, no matter the physical strengthen you'll need.

HypnoKinesthetics Case 8.

Donna was at the brink of being put on diabetic medication, which she desperately did not want. Through our HypnoKinesthetics sessions, she developed a new habit of exercising. She felt very proud of this accomplishment. She achieved some other goals during our work together as well. However, her addiction to sugar was still a daily struggle that seemed to dictate every spare moment in her obsession with sweets. HK allowed her to find the cause of that addiction, realize and forgive herself for this self-protective behavior, and find the solution to the sugar problem through movement and release it.

12:
YOU CAN
CHANGE YOUR DESTINY

"What inflicts the mind, inflicts the body. What inflicts the soul inflicts the body. Physical wounds heal much quicker but spiritual, emotional and spiritual wounds takes much longer of healing."
- Ann Marie Aguilar

Does your DNA contain the blueprints for who you are and whom you'll become? We used to think our DNA was a fixed inheritance from our ancestors. However, research debunks these outdated beliefs and puts us in the driver's seat of our destiny. *Genetic Determinism* is a flawed theory, and it's been widely known for decades.

We now know through the field of epigenetics, the study of biological mechanisms that will switch genes on and off, that you can control the expression of your genes through your thoughts, feelings, actions, environment, personal habits, where you live, climate, what you eat, and even how you sleep.

You can control the expression of your genes through your thoughts, feelings, and actions.

HeartMath believes that your thoughts, feelings, and daily intentions are fundamental elements of who you are and what you can become. That's right! And that means that on a cellular level, you can change the expression of your DNA and control your destiny.

According to Bruce Lipton, Ph.D., "The distinction between genetic determinism and epigenetics is important. If the genes control our life function, then our lives are being controlled by things outside of our ability to change them.

This leads to victimization that the illnesses and diseases that are common in families are propagated through the passing of genes associated with those attributes. Laboratory evidence shows this is not true."

As scientific research continues to illuminate who you are and how your mind and body functions, the opportunity for your intervention and evolution is crucial.

HypnoKinesthetics Case 9.

As a successful business owner, Cathy struggled with disempowering thoughts and feelings. With HK, she physically eliminated them and replaced with confidence, clarity and personal empowerment. When asked her what she wanted to do with those feelings. She said push them out and send them to the moon. She physically took the feelings out of herself and threw them to the moon, replaced them with confidence, and noticed how great she felt.

13:
SUMMARY & INTRODUCTION TO
HYPNOKINESTHETICS TECHNIQUES

"The place of true healing is a fierce place. It's a giant place. It's a place of monstrous beauty and endless dark and glimmering light. And you have to work really, really, really hard to get there, but you can do it."
- Cheryl Strayed

You've learned from this research that everything you've experienced has been memorialized, downloaded, and stored in your physical and mental body. They are permanently etched in your cellular memories. Each time you allow yourself to re-experience negative, hurtful, or unhelpful memories and feelings associated with them, you strengthen the neural networks in your brain. Over time this creates an automatic response which intensifies with each repeated experience. In other words, you stay stuck and often retraumatize yourself.

Conversely, your body has a limitless supply of positive cellular memories you can use to improve performance, feel happy, and achieve your goals. Your body holds the key to a fantastic storehouse of learnings and wisdom, positive history, and resources for healing. It is the key to your success, health, and happiness. Using these HypnoKinesthetics techniques will help you design new and empowering responses so you can heal and transform your life.

14:
THE COMPONENTS OF
HYPNOKINESTHETICS

"Healing takes courage, and we all have courage,
even if we have to dig a little to find it."
- Tori Amos

The main components of HypnoKinesthetics are:

- TimeLine Therapy

- Coaching

- Neuro-Linguistic Programming (NLP)

- Hypnosis

- Somatic Syntax

- Spatial Anchoring and Sorting

What's TimeLine Therapy?

TimeLine Therapy™ was developed by Dr. Tad James and Wayatt Woodsmall in 1988.

TimeLine Therapy™ is a system for creating powerful changes in thoughts, emotions, and behavior based on the principle that we have our internal timeline and unconscious storing of memories depicting our past, present. and future

It is a system for creating powerful changes in thoughts, emotions, and behavior. This system is based on the principle that we have an internal timeline and unconscious memories depicting our past, present, and future. This system is used successfully by psychiatrists, psychologists, marriage and family counselors, social workers, life and business coaches, and even athletic coaches.

Using Timeline Therapy™, you can change and alter memories of the past and present and create new memories of the future. The ability to change memories is extremely helpful in healing emotional traumas and eradicating unwanted thoughts, emotions, and behaviors. This system allows you to make these changes instantly rather than days, months, or years.

What's Hypnosis?

Hypnosis is a state of focused attention, reduced peripheral awareness, and an enhanced capacity to respond to suggestion.

Hypnosis is a state of focused attention, reduced peripheral awareness, and an enhanced capacity to respond to suggestion.

Hypnosis is a state of focused concentration, an altered or daydream state. It's similar to the state you experience when driving down the road while not remembering the drive.

You quite naturally get lost in your thoughts about either past or future events when driving, taking a shower, gardening, painting, running, fishing, watching TV, or reading a book.

During these activities, you leave the here and now while mentally participating in whatever you happen to be thinking about. You are in and out of trance all day long. You often get your best ideas while in the shower, driving or when waking in the morning.

Daydreaming is similar to being in a light state of hypnosis.

That trance state is a normal and natural state. It's how your mind works. However, this trance state is a very powerful state for making changes in your life. When you're in a hypnotic trance, you're the most receptive to ideas and suggestions. This receptivity is the reason hypnosis is such a highly effective therapeutic tool that makes change easy and, in many cases, permanent.

Hypnosis is an ancient, extremely safe, and highly effective process for personal change and healing.

Hypnosis has been successfully used for years to help in many areas such as surgery, childbirth, dentistry, weight loss, smoking cessation, as a remedy for insomnia, pain, chronic medical problems, anxiety, phobias, stress, confidence-building and nausea from cancer treatments and many others. It has been used quite successfully in the sporting world for many years and proven effective to enhance sports performance.

It's completely safe, and there are NO side effects! Hypnosis can be instrumental in helping you more easily make the changes you've struggled with for years.

Many describe the state of hypnosis as feeling profoundly relaxed and having a heightened awareness at the same time. You can come out of hypnosis at any time by opening your eyes. You are in complete control.

However, you don't have to have your eyes closed and relaxed to be in hypnosis. We use hypnosis quite successfully with athletes while they are actively performing their sport.

What's Coaching?

The International Coach Federation (ICF) definition of coaching:

Coaching is "partnering with clients in a thought-provoking and creative process that inspires them to maximize their personal and professional potential, which is particularly important in today's uncertain and complex environment."

In HypnoKinesthetics, we use the trance state in hypnosis to help the client access the problem and resources states. NLP offers a framework and movement patterns to support the change work. And Coaching skills allow us to move the client through various change processes.

Coaching differs from therapy, consulting, and even sometimes hypnosis work. In these systems, the practitioner is often the expert who advises the client what to do.

In the coaching relationship, the coach creates an environment that supports the client in increasing self-awareness. Coaching helps the client discover and give meaning to their solutions by using carefully crafted open-ended questions and following the ICF Core Competencies.

In HypnoKinesthetics, the practitioner holds the space within which the client learns to access, resolve, heal, and discover new solutions to challenges. We use the ICF, Core Competencies (Appendix C) as a guide in working with clients using HypnoKinesthetics.

What's Neuro-Linguistic Programming (NLP)?

Neuro-Linguistic Programming is a system of personal development that includes three powerful components involved in producing human experience: neurology, language, and programming.

Richard Bandler and John Grinder created Neuro-Linguistic Programming (NLP) in the 1970s. It describes the dynamics between mind (neuro) and language (linguistic) and how their interaction affects the body, mind, and behavior.

In NLP, your neurological system regulates how your body functions; Your language determines how you interface and communicate with others. And your programming determines the kinds of models of the world you create.

The basic foundation of NLP is that your words reflect an unconscious perception of yourself and the world. Some of these perceptions may be inaccurate or based on trauma or early life experiences, which may no longer be valid.

Some of these perceptions may carry unresolved and unhelpful memories and emotions. If left unchanged, these words and perceptions can contribute to ongoing problems.

The basic principle of NLP is that you can make positive changes in your unconscious programming to improve your responses. This allows you to heal from trauma, anxiety, fear, phobia, and improve your overall health and wellbeing.

NLP is one of the most effective and widely used skills used in sales, business management, psychology, sports, health, and personal development.

In HypnoKinesthetics, NLP is used to access and transform limiting, harmful, and destructive thoughts, feelings, and actions into effective and empowering new ways of living.

What is Somatic Syntax?

According to an old New Guinea proverb, "Knowledge is only a rumor until it is in the muscle."

This saying defines one of the basic premises of Somatic Syntax. Judith Delozier and Robert Dilts developed the term Somatic Syntax in 1993 as a way to further deepen and utilize the 'mind-body' connection.

In Greek, Somatic means, soma, or body. The Syntax is the Greek word that means "to put in order or arrange." Somatic Syntax means to organize our physiology and body language.

One of the primary objectives of Somatic Syntax is to mobilize and utilize the "wisdom of the body." A fundamental principle of Somatic Syntax is that there is 'information' in the body and 'knowledge' in 'the muscle.' Somatic Syntax primarily uses the movement of the body as a way to strengthen, integrate, and generalize deep level resources. By exploring the physical form and organization of the movements associated with a particular state, we can learn to better express or manifest that state in more situations and increase our flexibility.

What is Spatial Anchoring and Sorting?

Spatial Anchoring is a term that refers to creating an anchor to a physical location. This means you can anchor a particular state to a physical location, for example. Then, later, whenever you want to access that state, you can do so quickly by returning to that physical location. We use Spatial Anchoring to cleanly separate different states to allow more manageability of each state as a distinct entity. They are also called psycho-geography.

Spatial Sorting involves placing different internal states, beliefs, cognitive processes, or "Parts" of a person into separate physical locations. The technique was modeled based on the work of therapists Fritz Perls and Virginia Satir. They who routinely used different physical locations to help people to access, distinguish, and establish communication between conflicting or contradictory "parts" of themselves. It was the basis of Perls "empty chair" technique, for instance, in which he would have clients change chairs as they enacted conflicting thoughts and emotions. Virginia Satir used spatial Sorting as a key element of her "Parts Parties," associating different internal parts with specific physical locations surrounding the person.

15:
IMPORTANT
TERMS & CONCEPTS

"I am not my body, although I inhabit it, I am not my mind, although I use it as a tool. And I'm definitely not my opinions or beliefs, they are just things that I hold."
- A. Antares

Before examining these techniques, let's review a few terms and concepts used repeatedly throughout.

Inner Resources:

These techniques are based on the premise that you have many untapped internal resources (skills, talents, abilities, and feelings). You can locate, mobilize, and use these resources to help you resolve problems, feel better, and achieve your goals.

You may be aware of some of these resources consciously. For example, you may know that you can stick with something until it's completed or that you have the confidence to perform a particular function. Or you may not be aware of these inner resources located in the unconscious part of your mind. But imagine, being able to use the memory of excelling at something, being determined and relentless, or being able to express love, compassion, comfort, and encouragement as resources for achieving your goals.

These are inner resources you can re-use in other areas of your life too. Examples of inner resources or resource state include: Confidence, energy, motivation, determination, calm, and patience.

Mapping across:

You can use (transfer) the state of confidence you feel while playing a sport, singing, playing an instrument, or driving a car to another goal in your life. Doing this can help you feel more confident in public speaking or learning something new. Your mind knows "how to be confident." In NLP, we call this "mapping across," using one ability to share with another area.

More About Timeline:

Many of the techniques in this book use intuition, imagination, visualization, and an NLP concept called a *Timeline*.

Based on the idea that we organize time spatially, a Timeline is a system of viewing one's life from the perspective of past, present, and future.

It's a visual, linear experience of how you internally represent time. Even though we may represent our timelines differently, there are commonalities.

For example, when asked to "point to" where you see, sense or imagine a past event, like a favorite childhood memory, many people will point behind them or off to the right or left. You may see a future event, like the next season as being in front of you or to the right or the left. There's no right or wrong way of doing this.

However, in using some of these techniques, you'll be asked to "imagine your timeline" (usually on the floor or somewhere around you) with the past, present, and future in designated areas, while placing specific life events on it. This means that you'll be asked to move in a linear path, thinking forward and backward through your life as you imagine your past, present, and future.

In many of these techniques, you will be asked to go inside yourself (think about) and find a feeling or memory. Sometimes it's helpful to close your eyes while doing this. If you're standing, you may need to hold on to something to balance yourself.

Giving yourself permission to see, sense, imagine, or even pretend and trusting the process will serve you well while engaging in these techniques.

Mental Rehearsal:

A Mental Rehearsal is a technique that has been used widely in sports to enhance performance. Before the body can do an action, the mind must first see the action being done. This "seeing" is at the core of every great invention, performance masterpiece, and other significant accomplishments.

When performing these techniques, always trust your instincts, intuition or gut, and the first idea, feeling, and movement that emerges. Doing so allows you to access the unconscious knowledge inside you before your rational, thinking, and often self-critical mind interjects and starts to control the way you do the activity.

Finally, as you work through, resolve problems, and gain positive resources, remember that you have a brilliant and magnificent mind. It's your greatest asset and resource.

I've worked with thousands of people during my career. One of the most important things I've learned is that learning to use the power of your mind is the key to success in any area.

You can have the best education, a million-dollar house, and an outstanding reputation. But if you don't believe you deserve it and you feel unworthy, undeserving and lack confidence, you can remain stuck and unhappy.

Those thoughts, feelings, beliefs, and behavior are not who you are. They are often temporary states of being or inherited beliefs, and they're changeable.

Chakras: See Appendix A

Affirmations: See Appendix B

Visualization: See Appendix B

Music Titles: See Appendix B

ICF Coaching Core Competencies: See Appendix C

Anchor:

In this context, an anchor is the deliberate linking of a resource (memory or state, like confidence, calm, happiness) to a stimulus (anchor) so when triggering the anchor, the resource state is activated. For example, you can link your past inner resource of confidence to a specific movement or gesture (anchor) like pressing thumb and index finger together. This anchor can be used to help you overcome nervousness just before giving a speech.

Anchoring lets you use your inner resources whenever you want them. With anchoring, you can replace unwanted feelings and thoughts with desirable ones, gain control over emotions, and access memories and creativity. You can generate visual, auditory, kinesthetic, olfactory, and gustatory anchors.

Unhelpful state:

Unhelpful states are emotions like feeling nervous, depressed, anxious, or angry, for example. While all emotions are useful at some point or another, in HK they are termed unhelpful when interfering with a goal.

HypnoKinesthetics Case 9.

Stacy C had the opportunity to explore a new career, her dream job in another state. It meant additional expenses and the possibility things wouldn't work out. One part inside her was afraid she wouldn't make money and would go into debt. Another part of Stacy was ready and excited to go for it. Through HK, Stacy learned what the positive intention for her was for each part through their behavior. She used her body to express this process in movements and was able to cancel and clear the fear completely.

16:
USING HYPNOKINESTHETIC TECHNIQUES

"The body is a self-healing organism, so it's really about clearing things out of the way so the body can heal itself."
- Barbara Brennan

I've based these techniques on mind-body research. They have a history of successful application with clients, students, and myself who have benefited immensely by using them.

You will discover some new, some old, and some revised techniques that use movement in the therapeutic resolution of challenges. Even though you may be accessing visual and auditory information, these techniques are generally feeling-oriented or kinesthetic movement based in nature.

The formatting of this book allows you to locate a technique quickly, review it, and use it for yourself, your private clients, or in group training. Use them and enjoy!

1: HK FOR MORNING-EVENING RITUAL

Purpose: To connect with ourselves mindfully with intention and purpose as we begin and end our day.

Author: Patricia Eslava Vessey

Background: Using this daily ritual help us stay grounded, centered, and focused on our goals as we face a sometimes-unpredictable day. The evening ritual helps us release unhelpful thoughts and feelings accumulated from the day. These rituals create anchors in our body, which can override former, unhelpful patterns.

Steps:

Morning Ritual:

1. As you awaken, go inside yourself and think about the day ahead.

2. Ask yourself, how do I want to "be" today? How do I want to think, feel, and perform throughout my day? As you answer these questions, allow any positive images, sounds, and good feelings to emerge. Let these desired feelings and thoughts intensify and grow stronger and stronger. Then allow your body to create a movement or gesture that represents these feelings and thoughts you want during your day. Repeat this movement or gesture 3-5 times and throughout your day. How did that feel? I hope it felt good.

Evening Ritual:

1. As you prepare for sleep, think about what thoughts, feelings, and actions you want to release from the day. Go inside yourself and notice where you feel them. How do they feel? Using your hands, pull them out of your body and dispose of them as you prefer, such as, shrinking them down, changing the image, removing the color, shape, sound, throw them down the garbage disposal, erase them, burn, extinguish or disintegrate, etc. Repeat to make sure they are gone.

2. Then think about the thoughts, feelings, and gratitude from your day that are good, valuable, and you want to keep? See, sense, imagine, and feel them in your body. Intensify the good feelings. Then create a movement or gesture (perhaps it will be the same movement or gesture over time) that represents these good thoughts and feelings. Repeat 3-5 times.

2: HK FOR SUCCESS

Purpose: To use the power of your imagination to increase your success using the power of your imagination.

Author: Patricia Eslava Vessey

Background: Learning how to reprogram your thoughts, remove roadblocks and step fully into the success you want will help you in many areas of your life.

Steps:

1. Think about the success you desire. This is something you know you want to do or be, and perhaps you've been holding yourself back from achieving it. You know you have the capability, but something is stopping you.

2. Rate your current level of success in this area, on a scale ranging from 1 (no success) to 10 (great success).

3. See, sense, feel and imagine this success you want and intensify these feelings. Notice where those feelings are inside. Then give that success you want a movement or gesture with your hands and say a positive statement about it as you perform the movement (#1).

4. Now think about the obstacles that have been holding you back. Notice where those thoughts, feelings or beliefs live inside you or where you feel it in your body. Give those obstacles a movement or gesture and say a statement to yourself about it as you perform the movement (#2).

5. Perform the first, then, the second movement while saying each statement three-five times.

6. Movement (#3) What will it take (inner resource) to allow you to achieve success? Go inside yourself and find a time when you experienced that inner resource. Relive it, intensifying the sights, sound, and feel of the experience. Express the resource in a movement or gesture.

7. Repeat all three movements and statements three-five times allowing any changes in thought, sound and feeling to emerge while thinking about what action you'll take next. See, sense, feel or imagine going through your day, week, month and years in a new way, feeling so much better now with the success you desire.

8. Re-rate and notice the difference.

3: HK FOR CONFIDENCE

Purpose: To create and increase confidence in daily living. Use this technique before a performance or event or whenever you need more confidence.

Author: Patricia Eslava Vessey

Background: Building confidence is the groundwork for success.

Steps:

1. Think about a future situation or event where you want to have more confidence.

2. Rate your level of confidence regarding this event right now on a scale ranging from 1 (no confidence) to 10 (highly confident).

3. Pick a spot in front of you, step forward into it, and remember a time when you were confident. Re-live the experience, seeing, sensing, feeling, and imagining as if it's happening now. Amplify by adjusting the sights, sounds, and feel of it while letting it grow bigger and brighter, stronger, and more vivid and alive.

4. Create a movement or gesture that expresses or represents it. Repeat the gesture two-three times.

5. Create another space in front of you and step into it, remembering another time that you felt confident. Amplify it (like before), and create a gesture that represents it. Repeat the movement three times.

6. Designate a third spot in front of you that represents another time you did something well, or you were recognized or acknowledged for something. Step into it amplifying and repeating the process and creating a third movement or gesture. Repeat the movement three times.

7. Step back into the last experience and repeat the gesture. Step back into the first space and repeat the gesture. Step forward and backward, repeating each gesture or create a movement or gesture that combines all three movements.

8. Imagine your timeline and designate places for your past, present, and future. Now, step into and imagine that future event where you want confidence. Perform all three movements as you see, sense, and imagine having more confidence in this situation. Repeat in future situations while feeling your confidence grow stronger.

9. Re-rate and notice the difference. If no difference, repeat until there is.

4: HK FOR MOTIVATION

Author: Patricia Eslava Vessey

Background: Building motivation is the groundwork for success.

Steps:

Note: You can lead someone through this by reading the script below.

1. Think about a future situation or event where you want to be more motivated to accomplish something. Maybe you want more motivation to exercise, complete a project or start something new. Bring that situation to mind and imagine it as a picture, right there in front of you.

2. Rate your level of motivation right now on a scale ranging from 1 (no motivation) to 10 (highly motivated).

3. Now, remember a time from your past when you were very motivated. Re-live that experience noticing what you see, hear, feel, and maybe even taste and smell related to this experience. What does it feel like to be motivated? What is that feeling, and where do you feel that feeling in your body? Intensify this feeling.

4. Give that feeling a movement or gesture and a color if you like.

5. Take that motivation in your hands. Then, put your hands (with the motivation) through that picture and let go of that motivation. See, sense or imagine that motivation swirling through and saturating that picture and situation where you are increasing your motivation. Then, slowly bring your hands back out of that picture while letting that motivation stay there.

6. Physically step forward into that picture, perform that motivation movement or gesture, and notice how that situation has now changed as you are more motivated. Feel your energizing motivation in that picture, in that situation. Feel every cell in your body saturated with this motivation. See and feel yourself accomplishing your goal with that motivation you now have. Say something positive to yourself or hear the positive sounds that let you know you are now highly motivated.

7. Imagine other situations in the future and see yourself motivated in those pictures. Put that motivation where you want it in all your future pictures where. Then, step into those future situations and feel, see, and hear your energizing motivation increasing day by day. This energizing motivation is now helping you achieve your goal, feel better, more confident, more in control of your life, happier, and more successful.

8. Re-rate and notice the difference.

5: HK FOR TEAMS
(Work, Corporate, & Team Building)

Purpose: To build flexibility, inner resources, and cooperation within teams or in one-to-one sessions.

Author: Patricia Eslava Vessey

Background: Cultivating flexibility, patience, cooperation, empathy or other abilities in the way you respond enables you to work more productively and successfully with others. This technique can be used individually or in group team building sessions with discussion and feedback. Many of the other techniques can also be used with work groups and in team building too.

Steps:

1. Think of a future situation where you want three or more inner resources like being empathetic, patient and/or cooperative, for example.

2. Rate your current level of confidence in these three desired resources in this situation on a scale ranging from 1 (no confidence) to 10 (highly confident).

3. Designate three places on the floor that represent your chosen traits: i.e. Empathic, Patient, and Cooperative.

4.   Step into each place and recall a time you experienced it (empathic, patient, and cooperative). Notice what you see, hear, and feel. Also noticing where you feel it in your body and what that feeling is like. Intensify the feeling and allow it to be expressed in a movement or gesture. Move to the next place giving the feeling a movement, until you have completed all three.

5.   Then, go back through each one, reconnecting with the feeling/sensation and bringing it with you into the next place. Repeat immersing yourself fully and combining these resources.

6.   Allow a movement or gesture to emerge that represents all three combined, adding sound, image, and color if you wish.

7.   Return to the future situation where you want these abilities, i.e. to be more empathic, patient, and cooperative and perform the movement or gesture three-five times, as you see, sense and imagine yourself in that situation or event unfolding with you having these strengthened abilities. See, sense, feel and imagine yourself in future situations fully expressing these abilities and notice the positive results.

8.   Re-rate that feeling while considering what you will do differently now.

6: HK FOR HEALING

Purpose: To heal from emotional trauma or a chronic physical condition.

Author: Patricia Eslava Vessey

Background: Your mind-body is a powerful source of wisdom and resources that can help you heal and release trauma and transform thoughts, feelings and sensations.

Steps:

1.   Think of what you want to heal.

2.   Rate its effect on you (intensity, fear, frustration, discomfort, etc.) on a scale ranging from 1 (no discomfort) to 10 (very uncomfortable).

3.   Pick 4 places on your timeline: Past, Present, Future, & Resources.

4. Step into the Present place, and fully access your current feeling state that needs healing. See, hear, and feel everything about it, noticing where you feel it in your body. Allow a movement or gesture to express this feeling or state.

5. Step into the Past place, and see, sense or imagine what caused the need for healing (problem). There's a part of your mind that knows this. Trust your inner wisdom and go with the first thing that comes up. See, hear, and feel everything about it, noticing where you feel it in your body. Allow a movement or gesture to express this feeling.

6. Step into the Future place, and see, sense or imagine what you want and how you want to feel in place of or instead of that problem. What would that look, sound, and feel like if you experienced this instead of the present feeling? See, hear, and feel everything about it. Noticing where you feel this in your body. Allow a movement or gesture to express this feeling.

7. Move from the Past, Present, and Future expressing each movement, 3 to 4 times, creating a sequence.

8. Step into the Resource place to determine what inner resources are needed to support you in achieving your desired future. See, hear, and feel everything about it, noticing where you feel it in your body. Allow a movement or gesture to express this feeling.

9. Move from the Past, Present, and Future. First performing the movement or gesture representing that place. Then, adding the resource movement or gesture. Repeat as many times as you feel needed to shift your inner feelings about the problem. See, sense, feel or imagine going through your day, week, month and years in a new way, feeling so much better having released those old sensations.

10. Re-rate and notice the difference.

7: HK FOR STRESS

Purpose: To bring peace, calm, and relief from stress. Use this technique to create a daily practice to use in the morning and/or evening or before a stressful event.

Author: Patricia Eslava Vessey

Background: Cultivating the ability to create inner peace and calm is healthy and beneficial. It soothes the nervous system while giving you the message that everything is going to be okay. Use this tool daily and notice how much better you feel.

Steps:

1. Rate your current level of stress on a scale ranging from 1 (no stress) to 10 (high stress).

2. Designate a place on the floor, (or do this while sitting), to be your place of inner peace and calm. Go inside yourself and find a time you felt peaceful and calm. Maybe it was on vacation, at the beach, in the mountains, in your bed or somewhere else where you felt peaceful and calm. Or, remember something you witnessed, or just pretend or imagine creating a feeling of peace and calm in your mind and body. Notice what it feels like in your body-the sensations and where you feel them in your body. What lets you know that is peace and calm? If that peace and calm expressed itself in a gesture, what would that gesture be?

3. Perform that gesture now, three times as you stand in your place of peace and calm. See, sense and imagine yourself going through your day, week, month and year accessing and using this peace and calm whenever you want.

4. Make sure this designated place is mobile, and you can fold it up and take with you to use whenever you want.

5. Re-rate and notice the difference.

8: HK FOR PAIN RELIEF-CHRONIC

Purpose: To alleviate the chronic pain that doesn't need medical attention.

Author: Patricia Eslava Vessey

Background: Physical pain is your body's signal that there is a problem. Seek medical help when warranted and especially before using any techniques that might mask or cover up a sensation that needs medical attention.

Steps:

1. Go inside yourself and notice that discomfort.

2. Rate your level of discomfort on a scale ranging from 1 (no pain) to 10 (high pain).

3. Notice any images, sights, sounds, tastes, smells, colors, or symbols that represent that discomfort. Notice how that discomfort feels. Allow a movement or gesture to express this sensation.

4. How do you want to feel instead? Go inside yourself and imagine how this would feel. Include any sights, sounds, tastes, or smells. Allow this good feeling to grow stronger and stronger saturating every cell and fiber of your body with this feeling you want instead. Represent this desired feeling in a gesture or movement. Repeat three times. Move from the pain movement or gesture to the change gesture or movement three times.

5. Locate, gather, and breathe in that remaining discomfort, then exhale and release that it. Let it go. Repeat these, gathering the discomfort and releasing breaths three-five times.

6. As you feel the discomfort changing, and becoming softer, repeat the wanted movement or gesture three-five times. Then breathe it in and let it settle where that discomfort was, soaking and saturating your body with these good feelings. Repeat three-five times.

7. Now see sense and imagine yourself going through your day, week, month, and year, in comfort while repeating the breathing and movement or gesture when needed.

8. Re-rate and notice the difference.

Option: Imagine the special power room in your mind. Locate the dial that represents discomfort (pain). Reach out and turn the dial down one level at a time while feeling the discomfort change.

9: HK MOTIVATION TO LOSE WEIGHT (AVERSION)

Purpose: To provide additional motivation and support as you commit to your weight release goal.

Author: Patricia Eslava Vessey

Background: This technique is adapted from a popular hypnosis technique, High Road to Success. We are motivated to change behavior in several ways. Some are motivated through fear of consequences (extrinsically) if no action is taken. Others are motivated intrinsically and look for the benefits of their actions. This technique uses the adverse effects of not taking action as a motivational tool to help in changing thoughts, feelings and behavior.

Steps:

1. Think about your current challenges and difficulty getting or staying motivated to release weight.

2. Rate your level of motivation to change your behavior on a scale ranging from 1 (no motivation) to 10 (highly motivated).

3. Imagine your timeline: Past, Present, and Future. Locate the past, the future, and the present day.

4. Stand on the PRESENT day and see, sense, and imagine all the problems associated with not changing your behavior. Notice any current negative consequences of your present state of health, like diabetes, lack of energy, lack of motivation, and feeling out of shape. Notice how you feel and where you feel it in your body, and what that means to you. Give that feeling a movement or gesture.

5. Walk forward on your timeline to the point that represents ONE YEAR from now without any change in your behavior. Now, please close your eyes and imagine it's one year in the future and perhaps your health has declined, you've gained more weight, you have more aches and pains, and maybe you feel like a failure. Notice what your life is like at this point. See, hear, and feel just what your life will be like if nothing changes. Think of all the unhealthy food you've eaten over the last year whenever you've wanted. Remember what you told yourself to make it okay to overeat and not take care of yourself. Feel the consequences of knowing that you're continuing to harm yourself. Create a gesture or movement that represents this feeling.

6. Imagine that it's FIVE YEARS from now with no change. Walk to that point on your timeline. What's your life like? See, hear, and feel what it's like. Notice what you're telling yourself. Also, notice what your doctor, friends, and family are maybe telling you. Notice how much weight you've gained by not changing your behavior. Perform that gesture.

7. Now it's 10 YEARS with no change in your lifestyle. Walk to that point on your timeline, noticing how much weight you've gained. Notice how your health has deteriorated. Notice how hard it is to get around, how winded you are, and how worried you are about your health. Perform that gesture.

8. STOP! Now, imagine a second, parallel timeline that shows how you can easily, successfully, and permanently do, think, and feel whatever, it takes to release excess weight. Walk back to the place that represents the PRESENT on that parallel timeline.

9. Walk forward to the ONE YEAR point on this successful, parallel timeline. You've been exercising regularly and eating healthily, and you feel great! It's been far easier and more enjoyable than you ever thought possible. Notice what it's like to be healthier, to have lost some of that weight, to know you are making progress, and becoming healthier. Notice that you're feeling more confident and more in control of your life. You are highly motivated, and you've created new healthy habits, and you love it. Feel all the good feelings. If you were to give those feelings a gesture, what would it be? Create a gesture or movement that represents this positive, triumphant feeling.

10. Repeat this successful process walking to the FIVE YEAR and 10 YEAR point on this timeline. Repeat the positive gesture and add additional movements and gestures that represent your success. Notice how much more positive you feel in body, mind, and spirit as a result of taking good care of yourself. Notice how much weight you've lost.

11. Now, notice you were at a crossroad, and you can choose your path. The first timeline is familiar, comfortable, but jeopardizes your health, and it will keep you from being healthy, fit, and achieving your goal. The parallel timeline involves more work, more commitment, but it produces success, confidence, self-control, improved health and freedom, and so much more.

12. Decision time: It's time to choose which timeline to follow.

13. You have selected the parallel timeline. Step on that timeline and see, sense, feel, and imagine your success. Feel yourself creating new habits, and letting that motivation increase and grow stronger with every breath you take. Tell yourself positive statements about this path while performing the gestures that represent all those positive feelings and the success you are achieving. Give those positive feelings a color or symbol. Breathe that color in, and let it fill every cell in your body to overflowing with intense feelings of confidence, worthiness, motivation, determination, and everything you'll need to ensure you stay on that timeline.

14. Then, imagine before you that timeline of one year, five years, ten years, 20 years, 30 years 40, 50, 60 years into the future. Paint that entire timeline of yours with that color, seeing sensing and imagining that color flooding your entire future.

15. Then, walk forward on your timeline into your future, feeling empowered, confident, and happy you made an excellent choice for yourself, a healthy life. Feel these good feelings and let then sink deeply into every fiber of your body.

16. Re-rate and notice the difference.

10: HK - TRANSFORM RESISTANCE TO EXERCISE

Purpose: To eliminate resistance to exercising.

Author: Patricia Eslava Vessey

Background: Cultivating and engaging in an ongoing exercise habit is important, and not just for weight loss. There are countless mental, emotional, physical and spiritual benefits for moving your body each day. Exercise also helps to remove stored toxic stress and it can transform traumatic and painful cellular memories into empowered ways of living. Note: reasons for not exercise such as non-sufficient time can also be viewed as resistance. There are a number of ways to discover needed time for self-care.

Steps:

1. Think about exercise and the challenges you may have had starting and maintaining a consistent exercise habit.

2. Rate your level of difficulty and resistance to exercise daily ranging from 1 (no resistance) to 10 (total resistance).

3. Designate these five places on the floor (A – E):

    A. Exercise: Step into this place, think about and choose an exercise you could realistically incorporate into your life. This exercise is one you can be consistent with if the resistance was gone, and desire and motivation are present. See, sense, feel, and imagine doing this exercise. Create a movement or gesture to express this exercise.

    B. Benefits of exercise: Step into this place, think about, and list how engaging regularly in this exercise will benefit you. See, sense, feel, and imagine having these benefits and how this will impact your life. Feel these good feelings and express them in a movement or gesture.

    C. What will happen if no change? Step into this place and see, sense, imagine, and hear your self-talk if there is no change. How will you continue to feel about yourself? How will your weight, health and wellbeing be affected if there is not change? Is there any reason to keep these effects? Express these feelings in a movement or gesture.

    D. Think about the challenges and resistance that prevent your success with exercise. Imagine all those reasons, excuses, and distractions. Go inside and notice where that resistance lives. Find out if there is a message for you. Then create a movement or gesture to eliminate or move them away, i.e., pull them out of your body, shrink them down, drain the color and physically remove, reject, reduce and eliminate them with a movement or gesture. Repeat the movement or gesture.

    E. Resources: What inner resource (s) do you need that will assure your success? What does that resource look and feel like? Remember a time you experienced that resource. See, sense, feel, and imagine that time and let it grow bigger, stronger, and more powerful than ever. Allow your body to create a movement or gesture to represent it. Repeat this movement for three-five times (repeat this for other needed resources).

4. Step back into place A through D revisiting the respective thoughts and feelings and perform the movements. Repeat three times.

5.   Then step back into each place, repeating the movement or gesture, then adding the Resource movement or gesture. Repeat 3-5 times.

6.   Re-rate and notice the difference.

11: HK - SLEEP: SLEEP SUIT

Purpose: To achieve a deep, restful, and undisturbed sleep.

Author: Patricia Eslava Vessey

Background: This technique will help you get in your sleep zone.

Steps:

1.   Create a visual representation of a magical Sleep Suit created and personalized just for you. Imagine that Sleep Suit relaxes each part of your body, from the top of your head to the soles of your feet.

2.   Imagine dials, buttons and/or switches that adjust the comfort in your suit. Add elements that feel wonderful to you, such as, perfect temperature, soothing music or the voice of an angel (for example, telling you everything is going to be alright, relax, relax, relax, go to sleep or maybe you want them to sing to you). Perhaps you will add light massage or stroking of your head and body or a rocking motion. Maybe you want to add the feel of silk or softness, or water on your body. Add whatever is soothing and will help you sleep deeply and comfortably through the night. Give this Sleep Suit a color if that feels good. You can adjust them with the dials, buttons and/or switches, getting them just right so that you have complete and total comfort.

3.   See, sense, feel and imagine stepping into your Sleep Suit. Adjust the controls for complete comfort. Once you are ready, take hold of the sleep switch. Turn it on and lock it in place.

4.   Set this Sleep Suit next to your bed, or if you sleep in multiple places, make it a Sleep Suit that you can fold up and take with you wherever you go.

5.   When it's time to sleep, physically step into your Sleep Suit, adjusting the dials, buttons and/or switches, and climb into bed and go to sleep.

Note: This can also be a hypnosis sleep recording.

12: HK LEARNING FROM FUTURE SELF

Purpose: To gain inner wisdom, resources, and motivation for daily living.

Author: Patricia Eslava Vessey

Background: This technique provides knowledge from the unconscious mind by way of a message from your future self.

Steps:

1. Imagine your timeline, past, present, and future.

2. Step onto the present moment and think about something you want to heal, change or overcome (perhaps a destructive habit, belief or feeling). Notice how that feels, what the feelings are, and where you feel them in your body.

3. Imagine a time in your future, maybe days, weeks or months when this problem will be healed, released and is no longer in your life.

4. Walk forward on your timeline to that future place, allowing your best inner wisdom to take you there. See your future self in front of you. See, sense, and imagine what she/he looks like. What is it that lets you know she/he is free from that problem? Is it the way she/he is standing, their smile, their confidence? Notice what that is. Then, listen, because your future self has something very important that she/he wants you to know. Hear the message and tell her/him, thank you!

5. She/he has a gift she/he wants you to have that will help you on your journey. Reach out and take the gift. What is it and how will it help you?

6. Now, step forward into that future you and be her/him. See through her/his eyes, feel with her/his body, hear with her/his ears and truly know what it's like to know that you did get over it. That old problem you used to have is no longer an issue. It's gone from your life. Allow this feeling to manifest in a feeling or gesture.

7. Notice what your life is like without that problem. What are you doing, seeing, hearing, and feeling in that successful future?

8. Then, step out of your future self and back into your present you, bringing back all that learning, wisdom and knowledge.

9. Walk back to now.

13: HK - GETTING WHAT YOU NEED NOW!

Purpose: To gain resources needed at the beginning of your life to help you heal from the past and have resources for the present and future

Author: Patricia Eslava Vessey

Background: Timeline therapy is a powerful and effective way to help you release unhelpful memories, feelings and thoughts. You can transform your life using the power of your mind to re-imagine your life with everything you needed at the start.

Steps:

1.   Designate past, present, and future on your timeline. Walk back on your timeline to the beginning of your life at conception. Walk toward the present in a way that physically expresses what your life has been like, adding movements and/or gestures.

2.   When you get to the present, step off your timeline, and think about what you needed, perhaps at the start of your life for things to turn out better, more happily, more successfully, and to improve the quality of your life.

3.   Think about a resource that would have improved everything in your life if you had received it at the beginning. What is that resource? Notice what it is, then go inside and find a past experience of that resource whether it was something you experienced personally, you witnessed someone else do, or an experience you can imagine. Amplify that resource see, hear, and feel and let it grow bigger and stronger, more alive, more vivid, and more real. Create a gesture or movement to anchor that resource.

4.   Then, go back to the beginning of your timeline, reach down and pick up that younger you. Give her/him love, a hug, and the resource. Tell her/him everything is going to be alright. Then, walk through your timeline, performing the movement. Saturate every event with that resource, all the way up to the present time and into the future. Notice how that changes everything. See, hear, and feel the changes.

5.   Go to the end of your future timeline and look back at all the excellent work you did on your timeline. Using your hands, bring light into your timeline and color if you like. Integrate and update your mind with this new resource.

14: HK BODY TALK

Purpose: To connect with and learn from the wisdom of your body.

Author: Patricia Eslava Vessey

Background: We have much to learn and gain from understanding our body and giving it a chance to give us feedback through movement and dialog.

Steps:

1. Find a quiet place where you will be undisturbed. Have a pen and journal or paper on hand. Think of something to work on that is troubling you. Rate your level of unhelpful emotion or thought in this situation ranging from 1 (non-existent) to 10 (extremely strong).

2. Go inside yourself and notice what it is that is troubling you. Where in your body do you feel it? How does it feel? What are the feelings? Notice any sights, sounds, tastes and/or smells associated with it.

3. Begin to write to it, describing whatever you find yourself wanting to say. Just letting your pen run until there is no more to say and it comes to a complete stop.

4. As you do this, ask it the following questions: How have I treated you? What do I expect from you? What demands and commands have I've been making? What have I been ignoring and what will happen as a result? What would be better for me to do? What is your role? What should you be doing? How have you let me down? What is our relationship like? Continue to write until the writing is completed.

5. On a new page, invite that part of your body to write back to you. Again, let whatever words flow out from your pen to happen. Consider asking it the following questions. As you write, do so from the perspective of your body: What will happen if the current situation continues? What does it mean if the current situations continue? How do you want to be treated? What do you want from me? How can I help? How would you like our relationship to continue? What must never happen? What can happen instead? What else?

6. Continue this conversation until you find yourself arriving at some level of agreement and mutual accommodation.

Re-rate your level of discomfort/comfort. (1 low - 10 high)

15: HK FINDING THE INTENTION

Purpose: To connect with and discover the intention behind your behavior.

Author: Patricia Eslava Vessey

Background: Behind everything we do, even if it appears destructive like smoking, over eating, over drugging or giving in to cravings for example, lies a positive intention. Discovering that intention can help us find other, healthier ways to honor it.

Steps:

1. Think of some behavior, thought or feeling you've been engaged in that is troubling you. Maybe it's unhealthy behavior or perhaps it's engaging in an unhealthy thought or emotion.

2. Rate your level of discomfort, (1 low - 10 high)

3. Notice where in your body this "part" lives. Where do you feel it? Notice any sights, sound, tastes or smells associated with it. Relive the experience and see, hear and feel what that's like.

4. If that "part" were to express itself in a movement or gesture, that represented it, what would that movement be. Express the movement.

5. Ask the "part" what it wants for you by doing the troubling behavior, thought or feeling. Ask this "part" to express that positive purpose in a movement or gesture.

6. Thank the "part" for its purpose to help you. Continue to ask the "part", if you accomplish that purpose, what will that do for me that you want even more. Stop when you get a positive purpose.

7. Let the "part" know that the action it has chosen to meet that intention is no longer helpful Let the "part" know you want it to come up with another way (behavior, action etc.) to meet that positive intention that is truly helpful.

8. Ask the "part" to express this new action in a movement or gesture.

9. Repeat the movement or gesture 3-5 times.

10. Re-rate and notice the different feelings now.

16: KINESTHETIC TIMELINE REGRESSION

Purpose: To find the root cause of a past feeling or event to heal, change, resolve, and add resources.

Author: There have been many contributors to timeline regression. This is a kinesthetic adaptation.

Background: Historically, the first NLP techniques involving time were modeled from Milton Erickson, M.D. Erickson created his practical techniques based upon the well-known hypnotic phenomena of pseudo-orientation in time, otherwise known as regression (past) and time progression (future).

Steps:

1. Designate past, present, and future on your timeline.

2. Identify a problem event from the past that continues to trigger painful, unhappy, and unresourceful feelings.

3. Notice what you feel about that event. What are the feelings, and where do you feel them in your body? If you could represent the problem in a gesture or movement, what would it be? Perform that gesture or movement.

4. Starting at the present position, walk back on your timeline and perform the gesture noting similar feeling events, but not experiencing them.

5. Let your unconscious mind take you to the first event related to that feeling (where that feeling originated).

6. Note the event and step off your timeline.

7. What resources were needed that would have changed the event and experience in positive ways? Go inside yourself and find an experience of those resources (either experienced directly, witnessed, or created). Create a gesture or movement to represent it (stack all resources using the same movement). Create an affirmation.

8. Physically step into the original event first performing the unhelpful gesture, then the resource gesture. Walk forward to now, from the past, repeating the unhelpful and resource gestures.

9. Go back through your timeline, performing only the resourceful gesture and repeat the affirmation as you imagine walking through your future.

10. Repeat this process three-five times. Noticing the difference now that you have given yourself those resources throughout your history and into the future. What will you accomplish in the future now with those resources that were not available before? Savor the possibilities.

Variations: This kinesthetic timeline regression can also be performed to add useful resources that were not present from the beginning of your timeline. Resources that once added provide you with what you've been missing and that could help your life today (like feeling loved, cherished, capable, safe, protected, etc.)

17: HK GOALS FOR THE FUTURE

Purpose: To set your goal.

Author: Patricia Eslava Vessey

Background: The clearer you can be while setting your goal, the higher your chances of success. This technique involves a comprehensive, sensory experience of setting a goal.

Steps:

Think about a goal you want to achieve in the future. Choose a goal and answer these questions:

1. What's your goal? State it in the present tense. "I am now_____."

2. How will you know you have achieved it?

3. What will you be seeing, hearing, feeling, thinking, etc.?

4. What will happen when you have this goal?

5. How will achieving this goal affect your life?

6. Is it beneficial to me?

7. Is it beneficial for those around me?

8. Is there any reason you shouldn't achieve this goal?

9. Are you moving toward this goal or away from what you don't want?

10. When, specifically, when do you want this to happen? Set a date.

11. Now, create an internal picture that proves you achieved that goal. See, hear, and feel everything associated with that picture. Notice what you can see, state your goal and anything else positive, and feel the wonderful feeling of having achieved your goal.

12. Physically take that picture in your hands and walk forward on your timeline to the date you will achieve it. Take three deep breaths and exhale energy into your picture. Then, place your picture physically in your timeline; however, you imagine doing it.

13. Feel what it's like to have achieved your goal. Absorb it all into your mind and body.

14. Turn and walk back towards now, seeing, sensing, and imagining all the things you'll be looking forward to doing, thinking, and feeling to make sure you achieve that goal. Notice how the events between then and now realign themselves to support your goal.

15. Float back to now. Repeat this daily using visualization.

18: DESIRED BEHAVIOR – FINDING SOLUTION

Purpose: To find a solution while engaging in new behavior.

Author: Patricia Eslava Vessey (adapted from Michael Hall's technique)

Background: Using Spatial sorting and anchors will help you discover what's need to make changes and find solutions.

Steps:

1. Rate your level of confidence in finding a solution on a scale ranging from 1 (no confidence) to 10 (highly confident).

2. Designate four places on the floor to represent New Behavior, Outcome, Roadblocks, and Ideal.

3. Stand on "New Behavior" and think about a behavior you want to add or change.

4. Step on "Outcome" and answer these questions: Why do you want this? Why is it important to you?

5. Step on "Roadblocks" and answer these questions: What's preventing you from achieving your goal?

6. Step on "Ideal" and answer this question: What's more important than that roadblock, or what is a higher goal or ideal for you? Amplify this, see, hear, and feel the answers to these questions and put your hand over your heart as you amplify the feeling of this higher ideal and anchor it with your hand over your heart.

7. Now step back into the space of what holds you back, "Roadblocks," and put your hand over your heart and feel that higher goal.

8. Step back into why you want this goal space, "Outcome," and put your hand over your heart and feel that higher goal. Notice how it changes everything. What are you noticing? What are the changes? What new perspectives do you have? What new ways are you coming up with to achieve your goal? What adjustments are needed in your thinking, feeling, and behavior? How will you use what you're learning in the future?

9. Re-rate and notice the difference.

17:
HYPNOKINESTHETICS FOR SPORTS

*"Sports teaches you character, it teaches you to play by the rules,
it teaches you to know what it feels like to win
and lose-it teaches you about life."*
- Billie Jean King

You don't need to be an athlete to use these next three techniques. All you need is a strong desire to step up your game at work and in life.

19: HK - SPORTS & PEAK PERFORMANCE
(Excel at Sport-Stacked Anchors)

Purpose: To build confidence prior to a performance or event.

Author: Patricia Eslava Vessey

Background: Using successful events from the past and feelings associated with them will enhance your future.

Steps:

1. Designate past, present and future on your timeline.

2. Think about a future situation or event where you want to be at the top of your game, and where you want to be in the ZONE.

3. Rate your level of confidence in this future situation on a scale ranging from 1 (no confidence) to 10 (highly confident).

4. Recall a time from your past when you played or performed extremely well-the way you want to play all the time.

5. See, sense, hear, and feel the good feelings you experienced during that event. Intensify those feelings by doubling and then tripling them.

6. Notice where those feelings are inside your body.

7. If those feelings were to express themselves in a movement or gesture, what would it be? Create that movement or gesture, your Resource Anchor now. Repeat this movement three-five times.

8. Repeat Steps 1-7, adding two other memories (total of three memories) of excellent performance, adding them to the same physical movement for your Resource Anchor.

9. See your future game performance on your timeline.

10. Step on your timeline, walk forward to that future event.

11. Perform the movement, saturating the event with that Resource Anchor.

12. Walk forward through future events saturating them with the resource. See, sense and imagine your success.

13. Re-rate and notice the difference.

20: HK - SPORTS & PERFORMANCE
(Eliminate Pre-Game Anxiety)

Purpose: To eliminate pre-game/test anxiety. Make these techniques a regular component in practice sessions, performance preparation, before games, and, if possible, during performance breaks.

Author: Patricia Eslava Vessey

Background: Breathing patterns can be both calming and energizing. They calm mental clutter, put the body at ease, turn off the fight/flight, and freeze reactions giving you more self-control in the moment. Specific breathing patterns can also cause excitement, increase adrenalin, and prepare you for competition. These breathing patterns are associated with specific Chakras (Appendix A) for added focus.

Steps:

1. Think about a future situation where you want to be more confident (eliminate anxiety) and perform your best.

2. Rate your level of confidence right now in this situation on a scale from 1 (no confidence) to 10 (high confidence).

3. Using your full hand tap or pat on the following locations repeating the affirmation.

4. Root Chakra (earth element, located at the base of the spine-relates to the pelvic floor, legs, feet, and is grounding) while tapping on the base of the spine with the back of the hand, breathe in saying, "I am," exhale saying, "safe."

5. Third Chakra (fire element, located in abdominal region-relates to intuition, confidence, and self-esteem) while tapping on the stomach area, breathe in saying, "I am," exhale saying, "strong, confident, and positive."

6. Fourth Chakra (air element, in the heart region-relates to emotions, love, and compassion) while gently full hand patting-tapping over your heart, breathe in saying, "I," exhale saying, "love myself." Repeat with the sentence, "I support myself. I nurture myself."

7. Sixth Chakra (located at the third eye, middle of forehead region in front of the brain-relates to visualization and imagination) while tapping on the center of your forehead, see, sense and imagine your successful outcome and breathe in saying, "I am," exhale saying, successful."

8. Re-rate and notice the difference. Note: Also, use the Confident Technique.

21: HK - SPORTS & PERFORMANCE
(Zone-of-Success)

Purpose: To enhance your performance (to be in the "Zone-of-Success")

Author: Patricia Eslava Vessey

Background: Setting up inner controls that change your feeling, thoughts, actions and behavior can help you play better sports.

Steps:

1. Pretend you have a special "Control Room" inside your mind. Imagine there are many dials and that each dial has a name that corresponds to various emotions, memories, thoughts, and even bodily functions. Each dial has a range of intensity ranging on a scale from 1 (no intensity) to 10 (strongest intensity).

2. Find the dial marked "Zone of Success." Remember a time when you played exceptionally well, played in your "Zone of Success," and that you'd love to be able to repeat whenever needed. Maybe it felt like everything around you disappeared and you "became" what you were doing, and the outcome was extremely successful.

3. Now, go inside yourself and see, hear, and feel that event where you were playing in your "Zone of Success." Step into it and notice how and where you feel it in your body.

4. Reach out (physically) and turn up that dial marked, "Zone of Success." As you turn it higher, feel those feelings getting stronger and more powerful. Then, lock that dial where you want it to be. See, sense and imagine your success.

5. Select two more similar times when you were in your "Zone of Success" and repeat steps 2-4 above.

6. Repeat turning the dial down for any unhelpful emotions, thoughts and behavior.

18:
HYPNOKINESTHETICS FOR KIDS

"The greatest legacy one can pass on to one's children and grandchildren is not money or other material things accumulated in one's life, but rather a legacy of character and faith."
- Billy Graham

The next six techniques are intended for children, but some are used for adults as well. This chapter will focus on helping children to achieve healthy self-love, manage their stress and fear, enhance their ability to learn, and to create positive affirmations.

22: HK FOR KIDS:
(Confidence - Healthy Self-Love)

Purpose: To give children an inner, positive resource to use during tough times.

Note: This technique can be used for all ages including adults.

Author: Patricia Eslava Vessey

Background: For the most part, children can access these kinesthetic or feeling states much easier and quicker than adults. Cultivating a healthy or positive self-regard at a young age will build resiliency in children. This will be a much needed, very important, and lifelong inner skill and resource.

Steps:

1. Think about a time when you felt bad about yourself (maybe you felt unloved or not important).

2. Rate that feeling in this situation on a scale ranging from 1 (not bad) to 10 (very bad).

3. Think about the love or affection you feel for someone else like a beloved pet, toy, game, object, sibling, parents, or a best friend. Or, think about the love you've seen or witnessed on TV or in real life, or love that you can imagine in your mind. Or think of something you love doing.

4. Notice how that love feels and where it lives in your body. Notice if there are any images that come to mind. Notice any sounds or positive words you are saying to yourself about that love. Immerse yourself in that feeling of love, sensing all aspects of it. Intensify these love feelings, letting them grow stronger, doubling and tripling them.

5. If that love were to express itself in a gesture, what would that gesture be? Perform that gesture three times feeling that love. Now breathe that love into yourself. Let it settle into every fiber of your being, mind, body, and soul. Repeat this gesture three to five times.

6. Pretend and imagine there is another "imaginary you" standing in front of you. Then, physically give that love to that "imaginary you." Shower her/him with overflowing love, while imagining that love being absorbed by that "imaginary you."

7. See how it changes her/him. Perhaps there's a confident smile, posture or radiance about her/him. See how that love changes and improves everything in that "other you's" life. Notice and hear the positive things she/he says to herself now and notice the loving behaviors she/he takes toward her/himself etc.

8. Now, step forward, fully into that "imaginary you" standing in front of you fully becoming that you. See everything that future your is seeing. Hear with your ears, and feel those new and welcomed feelings of self-love, self-compassion, and self-care now and into the future. Let these feelings of love grow stronger and stronger. Step back into your current self and bringing that self-love with you.

9. Imagine yourself in future situations, some of which may be challenging. Feel the love. Feel the self-compassion for yourself regardless of what others say and do.

10. Repeat and re-rate.

23: HK FOR KIDS:
(Super Power for Thoughts & Feelings)

Purpose: To help children learn to manage their feelings.

Author: Patricia Eslava Vessey

Background: Learning to mastering self-management techniques will build resiliency in children especially during tough times. These skills teach self-control and self-empowerment. Teach kids that it's ok to feel their feelings. Sometimes the feelings can be unhelpful and they can learn to access the powerful part of their mind to help them control, change and manage their feelings, thoughts and behavior.

Steps:

1. Go inside yourself and find that unhelpful thought or feeling, whether it's anger, stress, frustration or something else.

2. Rate the strength of this thought or feeling on a scale ranging from 1 (weak) to 10 (really strong).

3. Notice where the thought or feeling lives inside your body. Notice how it looks (colors, images etc.). Notice how it feels, and what effect that thought or feeling has on you and your life. How and when does it show up in your behavior?

4. Are you ready to change that thought or feeling? Using that powerful part of your mind and your body, reach in and take that thought or feeling out of your body. Then drain all the color out, shrink it down so it's tiny and you can blow it away just like you would blow out candles on a birthday cake. Do that now.

5. Now that you eliminated that thought or feeling, what thought or feeling do you want instead of that old one, happy, silly, calm, confident for example? Go inside yourself and remember a time you felt this wanted feeling and had this thought. Remember how it felt, what you were doing and any sounds you heard. Then, using this powerful part of your mind, make this feeling bigger and brighter and awesome, and give it super powers. Create a movement or gesture that expresses this feeling now. Do that now. Repeat this movement three to five times as you imagine all the future times you will use this new super power.

6. Re-rate and notice the difference.

24: HK FOR KIDS:
(Calm, Centered & Relaxed in the Moment)

Purpose: To help children build flexibility, inner resources, cooperation with teams or in one-to-one sessions.

Author: Patricia Eslava Vessey

Background: Cultivating flexibility and inner resources in the way we respond allow us to work more cooperatively and inclusively with others. It can be used individually or in group team building sessions with discussion and feedback. This technique is based on Vorland's relaxation technique which focuses on relaxing the muscles most closely associated with stress and tension. For restless children, it's an effective distraction while interrupting an unhelpful state. It also teaches body awareness and self-control. Repeat this sequence several times to create a calm, relaxed, and focused state. Be sure to take slow, deep, and relaxing breaths in between each muscle group contraction.

Steps:

1. Toes: Curl your toes inside your shoes or against the floor, hold it and count to 10. Then, relax and breathe slowly and deeply. Feel the tension in your toes and ankles melt away.

2. Buttocks: Tense your buttocks tightly, elevating the pelvis slightly off the chair. Hold for 10 seconds. Then, relax and breathe slowly and deeply. Feel the tension in your buttocks melt away.

3. Fists: Clench your hands into fists while counting to 10. Relax. Feel how your hand and arm muscles relax and become heavy.

4. Shoulders: Tense your shoulders while counting to 10. Let go, relax and breathe. Feel the muscle tension melting away.

5. Jaws: Clench your jaws, tighten your lips while counting to 10. Relax your jaws and lips, breathe slowly in through your nose, and out through your mouth. Feel your jaws relax and become heavy.

6. Nostrils/eyebrows: Now, flare your nostrils and wrinkle your eyebrows while counting to 10. Relax.

7. Fists/jaws/nostrils/eyebrows: Clench fists, jaws, flare nostrils and wrinkle your eyebrows. Hold for 10. Now, relax and breathe.

8. Now, tense all the muscles from Steps 1 - 7, one after the other. Hold it and feel the tension. Now, relax and breathe. Feel the tension melt away.

25: HK FOR KIDS:
(Stepping Stones for Learning)

Purpose: To help children learn more easily.

Author: Patricia Eslava Vessey

Background: Cultivating study and learning tools will help children in school and independent study. It will also teach confidence and self-empowerment. This adapted NLP pattern is based on Robert Dilts, NLP pattern for accelerated learning. This pattern uses the chaining of experiences into a sequence for efficient learning that leads to a useful state. Use the experiences as transitional states to move you from a problem state to a resource for one.

Steps:

1. Think about a time when you had difficulty learning something - something you wanted to learn but it was a struggle.

2. Rate your level difficulty in this situation on a scale ranging from 1 (easy) to 10 (very difficult).

3. Remember a positive experience of a time you were excited to learn something. Re-live it seeing the sights and sounds and remembering the feelings of that positive experience (like excitement, motivation, being in the zone, being able to see, hear, and feel what you were learning).

4. Think of the first feeling you felt during this good learning experience. What did you notice first? Did you feel excitement, happiness, motivation or something else? Place this feeling on a stepping stone on the floor in front of you. Then, remember the next thing you felt. Maybe it was joy about how you would use what you learned. Place this feeling on another stepping stone in front of the other one. Find another feeling you had when you were learning something and it was fun and place that feeling on another stepping stone. Repeat for all the good feeling you experienced as you were learning something new. Questions to help are, how did you feel? What did you tell yourself? What did you do?

5. You can use actual stepping stones or something else like cardboard and write the feeling on each stone. Place them in an order in front of you. Step forward on the first stone and remember and feel that good feeling. Repeat this for each step remembering the good

feelings of the positive learning experience while anchoring each of these sequenced steps. Repeat 3-5 times.

6.   Now, think about the challenging learning situation while stepping on each step. Bring the challenging learning issue to mind. Move through each step while holding this in your mind. Go through the steps a few times if possible before you are back in the challenging learning situation.

7.   Test. Next time you're involved in the challenging learning situation, see how this pattern has changed your experience of this learning. Repeat 3-5 times and re-rate.

26: HK FOR KIDS:
(Improving Performance)

Purpose: To help children increase self-awareness of their current unhelpful actions while discovering and creating a successful future.

Note: Appropriate to use with adults.

Author: Patricia Eslava Vessey

Background: Learning to self-reflect is a valuable skill for kids. To be able to compare what they want and don't desire can help to form goals and the necessary traits to achieve them. This can help in school and relationships with self and others. It will also teach confidence and self-empowerment.

Steps:

1.   Think about a current situation where you are not performing as you want. Rate your level of "not performing" in this situation ranging from 1 (low achievement) to 10 (high achievement).

2.   Designate two places on the floor: one called "Current Performance" (this is something you are very good at, and it can be anything from feeding the dog to playing softball for example) and the other "Desired Performance" (this is something you want to improve, like doing your homework, chores or playing sports for example). Move between both positions answering these questions.

A Current Performance	B Desired Performance
I am good at **A** _____.	I want to be better at B_____
When I do **A** ___, I feel_____	When I do **B,** I feel_____
When I do **A,** I know_____	When I do **B,** I want to feel___
A is important because_____	**B** is important because_____
Being good at **A** means_____	Being good at **B** means_____
I'm committed to doing **A** because	I'm committed to doing **B** because

Picture, sense and imagine successfully doing B. Notice how that feels, where the feelings are and what that means to be successful with B.

My first step in doing B is_____

Re-rate and notice the difference.

27: HK FOR KIDS:
(Positive Walking Affirmations)

Purpose: To help children achieve a goal or gain new inner resources by training their unconscious mind. Also, for Adults.

Author: Patricia Eslava Vessey

Background: Affirmations (see Appendix B) combined with movement can become a powerful way to train your unconscious mind for success. It's also an effective way to combine exercise, meditation, and personal improvement. However, unlike walking, meditation is usually slower and includes mindfulness. Walking affirmations combines walking to the beat of each word or phrase in the affirmation. For example, using the affirmation, "I am happy," you can take a step on "I," another step on "am," and another step on "happy," or create your own rhythm, etc. This allows the words to integrate into mind and body. It's essential to write your affirmations and to spend time visualizing and creating a detailed (including sights, sounds, feel, taste, and smell) image or sense of yourself "being" that affirmation. You can also find music with the right beat and tempo and march, walk or jump to the music while stating or singing the affirmation.

Steps:

The definition of an affirmation is stating something that you assert to be true. See Appendix B.

To create your affirmation:

- Think about what you want and why you want it

- Think about the end goal you want because we tend to get whatever we focus on the most

- Your words have power

Here's a sample affirmation creating format:

- I am...

- I am willing to ...

- I am ready to ...

- I love it when ...

- I choose to feel safe and secure about...

- I'm grateful for...

- I expect to receive ...

---

1. Now, write your affirmation (*Appendix B*) to reflect your desired end-state that is meaningful to you rather than someone else. However, if borrowing an affirmation, make sure to add your sights, sounds, feelings, tastes, and smells.

2. After getting a clear internal representation, take a walk repeating the affirmations while stepping to the words of the affirmation.

3. Create anticipation and a feeling that your affirmation has come true.

4. With affirmations, repetition is the key to success.

5. Practice 2 – 3 times a day for 5-10 minutes or longer as you go for a walk.

19:
HYPNOKINESTHETICS
FOR QUICK HELP

*"We cannot teach people anything; we can only help
them discover it within themselves."*
- Galileo Galilei

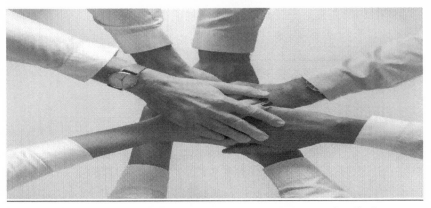

These five techniques can quickly help you to get unstuck, eliminate
unhelpful feelings, create healing metaphors, and change your mental state.

28: HK - QUICK HELP
(Feeling Stuck)

Purpose: To help shift your thoughts, feelings and sensations in the moment
or if you need a quick fix if you're feeling stuck. Though simple, this is a
very powerful technique that can provide quick relief. I use for headaches,
stress or feeling stuck when short on time.

Author: Patricia Eslava Vessey

Background: You have much more control over your thoughts than you may
know. This quick, easy, and powerful technique will put you in the driver's
seat in your mind while giving you the steering wheel to choose which
thoughts, feelings, and sensations you want.

Steps:

1. For a disempowering thought, see, sense or imagine that disempowering thought in your body.

2. Rate this disempowering thought on a scale ranging from 1 (no obstacle) to 10 (huge obstacle).

3. Using your hands, imagine taking ahold of the thought and you can either, slide it off to the left, squeeze it till it disintegrates, throw it at the sun and watch it burn up, grab it and push it over your head behind you, or any other creative movement that eliminates this thought.

4. Replace this disempowering thought with a positive uplifting and empowering one.

5. Then, either turn away or step forward away from it.

6. Repeat, rerate until it's gone And, replace that thought with a positive one.

Options:

Purpose: For unhelpful feelings and/or sensations.

Steps:

1. Go inside yourself and find that unhelpful feeling or sensation, whether it's discomfort, anger, depression, frustration, etc.

2. Rate that feeling in this situation on a scale ranging from 1 (no discomfort) to 10 (unbearable).

3. Notice where it is inside your body how it looks and feels, what effect it has on you, how you know it's a problem, how does it act, how does it react, what does it do to you?

4. How would you eliminate, change and/or transform this feeling or sensation? In other words, what do you want to do with that feeling or sensation that would feel so much better? Let your creative mind come up with ideas.

5. Perform that action now! Creating a movement or gesture that eliminates, changes and/or transforms that feeling or sensation. Repeat this action three to five times.

6. Re-rate and notice the difference.

29: HK - QUICK HELP
(Creating Healing Metaphors)

Purpose: To provide creative, fun, and playful ways to manifest problems or challenges to gain more knowledge and inner resources. Use this with children or adults. It can also be fun to do in groups.

Author: Patricia Eslava Vessey

Background: Using imagination and physical movement with this technique will bring added insight to resolving problems.

Steps:

1. Think about a time when you experienced a problem or disempowering unhelpful patterns, behaviors, feelings, or thoughts.

2. Ask, what animal (car, song, story, movie, etc.) does that problem move like?

3. Perform a movement or gesture that represents that animal, noticing how that feels in the body.

4. Notice what thoughts come to mind. What are you telling yourself?

5. What can you learn from this animal to solve this current problem?

6. What animal do you want instead that will eliminate that problem or transform it into something positive?

7. Perform that now, noticing how that feels, and what thoughts come to mind.

30: HK CHANGING STATES
(What in Life Makes You Most Proud?)

Purpose: To change unhelpful emotions and beliefs.

Author: Patricia Eslava Vessey

Background: If you change the mental state you're in, you'll shift those unhelpful emotions/beliefs. It will give you greater control over your thoughts, feelings, and actions. You'll be more successful when you can change your state at will.

Steps:

1. Bring up an unhelpful or unwanted feeling or thought. Focus on it and get a sense of how it affects your life.

2. Rate your level of discomfort is this situation ranging from 1 (comfortable) to 10 (very uncomfortable).

3. Go inside yourself and find something you are proud of, something you did, that made you feel good about yourself. Close your eyes and focus on how good that feels to remember something about yourself you feel good about. Think of something you can be excited about. See what you saw, hear what you heard, and feel those good feelings. Notice where in your body you feel those good feelings. Feel it and let these good feelings grow stronger and stronger and more vivid and enjoyable. Imagine a dial attached to these good feelings and turn this dial up so that these good feelings are incredibly strong. Then express these good feelings in a movement or gesture. Repeat three to five times. Enjoy these good feelings and keep them with you

4. Repeat, re-rate, and notice the difference.

31: KINESTHETIC NLP CHANGE PATTERN

Purpose: To change anything from the sensation of pain, anxiety, depression, stress, fear, and even habits.

Author: Patricia Eslava Vessey.

Background: This technique is based on the idea that everything is stored in sensory files inside our body. When you change the details of these files, it also changes the way they impact and influence you.

Steps:

1. Identify an unwanted feeling, behavior or thought you want to change.

2. Rate this feeling on a scale ranging from 1 (no discomfort) to 10 (unbearable discomfort).

3. Notice where in your body that feeling, thought or behavior lives.

4. Identify appearance, symbols, colors, shapes, sounds, feel, movement pattern and taste and smell of "it."

5. Physically reach in and pull it out, so it's in front of you.

6. Then, physically remove (using gestures) those descriptors.

7. Now, using gestures, re-create "it," so it feels good instead of the other identifiers.

8. Create or sculpt a new image, sounds, taste/smell, feel and move. Lock those changes in place.

9. Ask, would it be okay to keep these changes instead of the original?

10. Now, physically pull that new thing back inside where it was with those changes.

11. Re-rate and notice how it has transformed completely.

32: HK UNIFYING PARTS

Purpose: To create harmony, unity and focus between conflicting parts so you can achieve the changes you want.

Author: Patricia Eslava Vessey

Background: Underneath everything we do is a positive intention. Though not always apparent, and sometimes hidden under harmful and sometimes destructive behavior, this positive intention is there nonetheless. Sometimes when we want to make a change in our life, there's a part of us that wants the change while another part may be uncooperative, resistant, and unwilling to follow along. This resistant part's behavior can keep us stuck, unable to achieve the change we want. It can zap our energy, and contribute to an ongoing inner conflict between these parts that keeps us stuck. We can learn a lot from exploring these parts, discovering the positive intention, and creating a unifying partnership. Using the body in this process is a powerful way to reconcile parts, and it honors the intentions of both parts. The Ultimate Outcome for Me is defined as the end goal or outcome, how that part ultimately wants you to feel once it accomplishes its positive purpose for you. It can also be called the ultimate core state.

Steps:

1. Designate two parallel timelines one for the part that supports the change, and the other timeline for the part that resists the change. Designate Past, Present, Future, and Ultimate Outcome for You (UO4M) on the timelines.

2. Identify the problem, behavior, or response you want to resolve or change. Rate it on a scale, 1 (no problem), 10 (extreme problem)

3. Identify the parts in conflict. Part (S) Supports the change, and Part (R) Resists the change.

4. Focus on the part that Supports the change first (S).

5. Step onto the Present moment on (S)'s timeline.

6. Go inside yourself and locate where part (S) lives. Where does that part live? Notice what images come to mind, colors, or symbols associated with this part. Notice any sounds, smells, or tastes related to this part. What's the feeling associated with this part that supports the change? You can also notice the age of this part and if it has a gender and name if you like.

7. Allow that part to express itself in a stance that represents it.

8. Take one step forward on (S1) timeline while asking that part, "What do you want for me through achieving that goal?"

9. Go inside and find the answer and express it in a movement or gesture. Repeat three times, so your body remembers this movement.

10. Then, take another step forward on (S2) timeline while asking that part, "Once you've given that to me (previous answer), then what do you want for me?"

11. Go inside and find the answer and express it in a movement or gesture. Repeat three times so your body remembers this movement.

12. Then take another step forward on (S3) timeline while asking that part, "Once you've achieved that (previous answers) for me, then what do you want for me that's even greater?"

13. Go inside and find the answer and express it in a movement or gesture. Repeat three times, so your body remembers this movement.

14. Then, take a final step forward on (S4) and ask the part, "What do you want for me through having all of that (previous answers) that is your Ultimate Outcome for Me (UO4M)? How do you ultimately want me to feel in having what you want for me?"

15. Go inside and find the answer and express it in a movement or gesture. Repeat three times, so your body remembers this movement.

16. Go back to the Present position and repeat, stepping forward for each question and performing each movement. Repeat this sequence three times, ending with the Ultimate Outcome for Me movement.

17. **Now, go to the other parallel timeline for the Resistant Part (R),** Step on the Present moment position and revisit the problem you want to resolve and change.

18. Begin this with, "What do you want for me by resisting this change?" And repeat steps 6 through 16 (getting the moves for (R1,2,3,4) ending with the Ultimate Outcome for Me movement (UO4M).

19. Once you've repeated the resistant part (R) sequence of movements three times, go back to the present on (S) timeline and follow this sequence:

20. Perform (S1) followed by both (S) and (R)'s (UO4M) moves. Step over to (R) timeline and perform (R1) moves followed by both UO4M moves. Go back to (S2) and repeat this process, zigzagging from S to R timelines, performing the movements followed by the UO4M moves.

21. Repeat this "dance" three-five times

22. Re-rate.

20:
ADDITIONAL MOVEMENT BASED
NLP TECHNIQUES

"The truth is that there is no actual stress or anxiety in the world; it's your thoughts that create these false beliefs. You can't package stress, touch it, or see it. There are only people engaged in stressful thinking."
- Wayne Dyer

The next 14 techniques will help you relieve anxiety, release limiting beliefs, resolve problems, heal cellular memory, dissolve fear, change behavior, achieve goals, and replicate human excellence.

BILATERAL STIMULATION

Purpose: To relieve anxiety.

Author: This technique is the treatment element of the Eye Movement Desensitization and Reprocessing (EMDR). It was discovered by **Francine Shapiro**, Ph.D. as she was walking in a park in the late 1980s.

Background: Bilateral stimulation is stimuli (visual, auditory or tactile) which occur in a rhythmic left-right pattern. This technique stimulates both hemispheres of the brain which interrupts the pattern of anxiety. For example, visual bilateral stimulation could involve watching a hand or a light moving from left to right and back again. Auditory bilateral stimulation could involve listening to tones that alternate between the left and right sides of the head.

Steps:

1. Think of something that is causing you some anxiety.

2. Rate your level of anxiety on a scale ranging from 1 (no anxiety) to 10 (high anxiety).

3. Get a ball, apple or anything you can toss back and forth across the midline of the body.

4. Now pass the ball back and forth from one hand to the other, crossing the midline, so you are stimulating both hemispheres of your brain. It will have a more rapid effect if you keep one hand in front of you as the other swings out to the side each time you pass the ball.

5. Do this for a minute. Stop. Take deep breaths and check-in. You might note that the anxiety has dissipated.

6. Pass the ball (or another object) for a minute, and check-in. Repeat until the anxiety has completely gone.

7. Re-rate it again as you think of the same situation.

FASTER EMOTIONAL FREEDOM TECHNIQUE

Purpose: To help you release limiting beliefs, shift energy, and change emotions.

Author: Original contributor was, **Roger Callahan**, a psychologist. **Gary Craig,** a student of Callahan's developed Emotional Freedom Techniques (EFT) in 1995. He created his tapping techniques which involved tapping all the meridians points in your body. He added the reminder phrase, spoken as you tap each tapping point.

Background: Because Faster EFT is quick, easy, and powerful, I often teach this version to my clients, and I know they will use it. EFT combines cognitive therapy, voicing positive affirmations, the science of acupuncture, and mind-body medicine. It involves finger tapping on specific meridian points of the body to release stuck or blocked energy while stating affirmations. You can train your body and your mind to feel surprisingly calm and confident, no matter what. In this state, you have more self-control and access to choices you don't have when you're stressed. For example, you can choose to set and maintain healthy boundaries with others.

Steps:

Think about a time when you wanted more confidence, to release limiting beliefs, shift energy, or change emotions.

Rate your level of unhelpful emotion or thought in this situation ranging from 1 (non-existent) to 10 (extremely strong).

The tapping points: Tap each area with your fingers 5-7 times while thinking about the problem and stating, "I release it and let it go."

1. **Eyebrow point:** at the inner corner of the eyebrow, just above the nose.

2. **Side of the eye:** on the bone bordering the outside of the eye.

3. **Under the eye:** on the bone directly under the eye.

4. **Collar bone:** the junction where the collarbone, sternum, and ribs first meet.

5. **Hand on the Wrist:** say PEACE and feel the peace throughout the body.

This simple, quick, and easy technique will change your life if you let it. Avoid being discouraged if you don't "feel" a change right away. Remember, the EFT has been researched extensively and proven to work. So, stick with it. As you learn to tap, practice it often, and for various unhelpful thoughts, feelings, and ailments.

The more you use this powerful technique, the quicker you can use it when facing a challenge.

1. Bring the unhelpful emotion or thought to mind and rate it.

2. Re-rate and repeat until the number is 2 or under.

DANCING SCORE PATTERN

Purpose: To solve problems, change thinking, feeling, and behavior while discovering and using valuable inner resources.

Author: The SCORE pattern was created by **Robert Dilts and Todd Epstein in 1987.** The Dancing Score was developed by **Judith DeLozier** in 1993, as a means of using physical movement and spatial sorting to maximize intuition and the wisdom of the body in problem-solving. The format uses the Score Pattern and movement to create a series of movements or dance that lead the explorer from problem to resolution in a powerful and effective way. This is a modification/adaptation to the original dancing score pattern.

Steps:

1. Designate your Timeline: Past, Present, and Future.

2. Think about a problem you're trying to resolve. Rate it on a scale, 1 (no problem, 10 (extreme problem)

3. Designate five locations on the floor, in this sequence: Cause, Symptom, Outcome, Desired Effect (related to the problem), and Resources.

4. Step into and experience the "Symptom" location. Express this in a movement.

5. Step back into the "Cause" location. Allow the feeling and movement of the symptom to guide you to the cause of that symptom. Express the experience of the cause in movement. Notice any changes in the movement.

6. Step into the "Outcome" location. Experience and express this state in a movement.

7. Step forward into the "Desired Effect" location. Experience and express in a movement, the results of having achieved your outcome.

8. Walk through the entire sequence from "Cause" to "Outcome" expressing each movement. Go slow between the "Symptoms" and the "Outcome" and notice how your body connects these two spaces.

9. Repeat this several times as you link the moves together allowing (the dance) to unfold.

10. Go to the "Resource" location and discover resources to support this resolution. Experience and express the resource in a movement and add to the dance sequence.

11. Starting in the "Cause" location, incorporate the resource movement into the other movement associated with that location.

12. Walk through the other locations adding the resource movement to the other movements until you have reached the "Desired Effect" location.

13. Repeat the movement (multiple times) through cause/resource, symptoms/resource, outcome/resource, and effect/resource until you have transformed it into a kind of dance. Repeat dance multiple times.

14. Re-rate the problem

Options: Add music like, *"Beethoven's 5 Secrets"* or *"The Quality of Mercy"* by **Max Richter**.

ENERGY MEDICINE TOOL

Purpose: To heal your cellular memories, thoughts, and feelings.

Author: Dr. **Alexander Loyd**, Ph.D., N.D., a leading expert in the area of alternative medicine. Visit his website: thehealingcodes.com

Background: The Energy Medicine Tool can have a powerful effect for most people because it applies energy to specific points on your physical body to heal a symptom or a problem. It uses three positions: the **heart,** the **forehead,** and the **top of the head.** These areas house the physical parts of our body that directly affect (or are affected by) the stress response, and the control mechanisms for every cell in the body.

Steps:

For this position and for the others that follow, either: rest your hands in this position and hold for 1-3 minutes or move your hands gently in a circular motion in either direction, switching directions every 15 seconds.

1. **The Heart:** Stack your hands, palm down, on your upper chest (over your heart). This pours energy into your cardiovascular system and your thymus, as well as key energy medicine points for your immune system to induce cellular memory healing.

2. **The Forehead:** Stack your hands, palm down, over your forehead, with your little finger just beneath your eyebrows. Either rest your hands in this position for 1-3 minutes or, for faster results, move them in a circular motion moving the skin over the bones, switching directions every 10 to 15 seconds, for one to three minutes. This stimulates your entire brain: not only your higher and lower brain, but also your left and right brain. According to **Roger Sperry**'s split-brain experiments in 1972 (for which he won the Nobel Prize), the right brain includes our limbic system and our reticular formation, which govern wisdom, meaning, feelings, beliefs, action, and images. Our left brain governs words, logic, and rational reasoning only (i.e., no action and no meaning). You're also pouring energy into the third eye chakra (see *Appendix A*), one of the most powerful energy centers in the body. Also, according to Sperry's original research, the right brain may be one of the main control center locations of the spiritual heart, which is the "container" for our spirit: our unconscious, subconscious, conscience, and the so-called last frontier - everything else we don't even know about yet.

3. **Top of the Head:** Stack your hands, palm down, on the top of your head, or your crown. This position activates not only all the same physiological mechanisms of the forehead position (albeit from a different angle), but also the spinal column/vertebrae and the crown chakra, another powerful cellular memory point that governs your connection to the spiritual realm.

4. Re-rate and notice the difference. If no difference, repeat until there is.

This technique sends energy to all three areas, increasing blood flow and power to the control centers for every cell, every thought, every emotion, and every belief, as well as to your heart, third eye, and crown chakras (see *Appendix A*), the three most powerful cellular memory energy centers in the body.

HAVENING:
(NLP for Dissolving Fear, Mental Blocks, & Hesitation)

Purpose: To dissolve fear, mental blocks, and hesitation.

Author: Stephen J. Ruden and **Ronald A. Ruden.**

Background: Havening is an alternative therapy popularized in part by hypnotist and self-help practitioner **Paul McKenna.**

Steps:

Practice this useful technique until it becomes easy and quick to do.

1. Think about the mental block or obstacle that's holding you back. Rate it on a scale, 1 (no problem, 10 (extreme problem)

Now, clear your mind and think of something pleasant.

Next, use both hands and **tap on both your collar bones and:**

1. Keep your head still, look straight ahead, close & open your eyes.

2. Holding your head still, look down to the left and then down to the right

3. Keep your head still. Move your eyes in a full circle clockwise and then anti-clockwise.

4. Next, cross your arms, place each hand on the top of your shoulders and close your eyes.

5. Stroke your hands down the sides of your arms from shoulders to elbows and back again while imagining you are walking down a flight of stairs and count out loud from 1 to 20 with each step you take. When you reach 20, hum or sing the first two or three lines of Happy Birthday.

6. Let your arms go back down to your sides, relax, open your eyes and look up in front of and above you. Then, move your eyes slowly from left to right and back three times.

7. Close your eyes, breathe in deeply, exhale, and stroke your arms again in the same fashion a further five times.

8. Open your eyes. Repeat the exercise from beginning to end until the number is 2 or below.

You can also perform this exercise in almost any stressful situation like going to the dentist or before you are about to speak in public.

SPATIAL ANCHORING & SORTING

Purpose: To help you work through thoughts and emotions by cleanly separate different states so you can more effectively deal with each state as a distinct entity.

Author: The technique was modeled from the work of therapists **Fritz Perls** and **Virginia Satir**, who routinely used different physical locations to help people access, distinguish, and establish communication between conflicting or contradictory "parts" of themselves.

Background: Uses physical location to anchor and organize a particular state with a particular location. Later, when you want to access that state, you can easily and effectively do so by returning to that location (Also called *psycho-geography*). For example, go inside yourself and find a resource state, like confidence, energy, motivation, determination or patience.

Steps:

Spatial Anchoring: Designate a physical location to represent a state of mind.

Spatial Sorting: Places different internal states, beliefs, cognitive processes or "Parts" of a person into separate physical locations. Designate places on the floor that represents these "Parts." Step into one place and with *HypnoKinesthetics*, express it in a gesture. Get a positive purpose of the "Part." Repeat for the other part (s). Moving from one "Part" to the next while coaching a positive resolution and agreement to work together. You can use these concepts to change states, add resources, and positively affect beliefs.

NLP ANCHORING

Purpose: Anchoring is used to control your state, change your feelings, beliefs, behavior and achieve your goals, like losing weight, stopping smoking, overcoming the fear of public speaking, successfully interviewing for a job, improving performance and much, much more. It can be as easy as turning on a light switch.

Author: Based on the work of Nobel Prize-winning psychologist **Ivan Pavlov**, and later, **Milton H Erickson** who used his unique tonality to capture and deepen trance states in clients to effectively create change. **Grinder** and **Bandler** also contributed also and added this technique.

Background: An anchor connects experiences together, an internal experience with an external one, like the smell of apple pie and the warm feeling of being in grandma's kitchen. There are many examples of this powerful process, already in your memory bank. Have you ever noticed that when you hear an old song or smell something familiar that specific memories of sounds, tastes, smells or feelings are triggered? That's because your mind has consciously or unconsciously created an anchor for this experience.

Steps:

1. Decide what state you want to anchor. (i.e. confidence)

2. Recall a vivid experience for the state you're trying to anchor.

3. Apply a specific trigger before the state reaches its peak (i.e., press your thumb and index finger together, make a fist, touch your fingertips or some other movement)

4. Break the state: Think about something different.

5. Test and repeat the anchor until you achieve the experience you want.

CIRCLE OF EXCELLENCE

Purpose: To elicit, create, and stabilize desired states by using basic self-anchoring process.

Author: Originally developed by Dr. **John Grinder,** and Judith Delozier, co-creators of NLP.

Background: This technique uses a kinesthetic anchor to activate a moment of excellence, a moment in which you are at the top of your game, in which you feel like superman/woman.

Steps:

1. Choose a state of excellence that you want more of in your life (i.e., confidence, curiosity, peace, etc.).

2. Rate your level of confidence in this state of excellence on a scale ranging from 1 (no confidence) to 10 (highly confident).

3. While standing, imagine a large, colored circle on the ground in front of you. Let the color of the circle naturally represent your state of excellence (i.e., "my state is confidence, and I see that as purple.").

4. Let the imaginary circle represent a strong resource for your state of excellence.

5. Step into the imaginary circle of excellence and experience your resource state. Imagine the color of the circle surrounds you, and the resource state intensifies. Step out.

6. Think of a context that you would like more of your state of excellence in. As you begin to think about the context, step into the circle and re-experience the situation while in the state of excellence. Once that's fully integrated, step out.

7. Test. Imagine the context again and notice how it's different.

8. Repeat steps 6 and 7 for other contexts you want the state of excellence in as desired.

9. Future pace. Step into the imaginary circle of excellence. Imagine a few contexts in the future that are similar to the context (s) integrated into steps 6 and 7 and notice what they are like now with the resource state.

10. Re-rate and notice the difference.

SAD TO GLAD – CHAINING ANCHORS

Purpose: To enable state changes.

Author: Fran Burgess, NLP Cookbook

Background: Based on two premises: You can only hold a state for 90 seconds before it needs to be topped up by returning to whatever triggered it, and if you can go from happy to sad in that time frame, you can certainly go the other way as well. Also uses Somatic Syntax and Spatial anchors.

Steps:

1. Identify the state you don't want and the state you want instead. Identify states in between both that take you from the first to the last. For example:

   - Sad....Quiet....Content....Glad

   - Lethargic....Curious....Aroused....Alert

   - Unmotivated....Curious....Interested....Energetic

   - Rate your level of comfort with it on a scale, 1 (no problem) 10 (extreme problem)

   Place these states in a line on the floor with enough space to move from one to the next.

2. Step into the first space and allow your body to adopt a posture that fits that state, clear your mind and repeat, so you'll remember.

3. Repeat through all the states remembering each posture state.

4. Now, dance through each posture paying particular attention to each posture and allow the transitions to flow. Repeat several times.

5. At the final space, come up with a gesture that represents the feeling you now have. This can be your trigger to give you a boost when you need it.

6. Re-rate and notice the difference.

POWER STANCE:
(Change Physiology)

Purpose: To use when you feel stuck in a negative, limiting, or unhelpful state such (like feeling depressed, anxious or angry).

Author: Tony Robbins.

Background: Changing your physiology will change your emotional state. **Tony Robbins** taught this for many years. Harvard conducted a study which proves this and called it "Power Positions."

What they found was if you stand with your shoulders rolled back, hands on hips, elbows back, legs apart, similar to a Superman/woman pose, and breathe deep for two minutes, you will increase your testosterone by 20%. You can also drop your cortisol (stress hormone) by 22%, and you're 33% more likely to act on something you wouldn't have before - because your fear stopped you.

Steps:

1. Stand with your shoulders rolled back to change your breathing pattern. Place your hands on your hips, with legs apart - a strong "Power Position."

2. Speak more quickly to change your biochemistry, allowing you to take more positive actions.

3. Another similar state is to sit back with feet up and hands behind head (elbows out). This state will produce more certainty in you, which will help you take different actions.

4. Think about something you are excited about. See, hear, and feel what that's like. Then, make a sound to express that, create a gesture that expresses that. Repeat this for feelings of gratitude and other positive states.

VISUAL SQUASH TECHNIQUE

Purpose: To resolve internal conflicts.

Author: Richard Bandler, co-creator of NLP, is the original author of the *Visual Squash Technique* which is based on the work of Fritz Perls and Virginia Satir.

Background: This helps you resolve your internal conflict.

Steps:

1. Make an image of the two conflicting ideas/parts and place one in each hand. Create a mental image for each. See, sense, imagine, and feel the weight of each image in each hand.

2. Rate your level of internal conflict this situation ranging from 1 (no problem, to 10 (extreme problem)

3. What is the positive intention of each element of the conflict? What are they doing for you and/or making you feel?

4. Create a third image, which combines the good intention of the other two images, and imagine it hovering above your two hands.

5. Let your two hands join and merge (squash) the two images in your hands into this third image.

6. When you feel ready to make a change, bring your two hands towards your chest and absorb the third image into your body. Let that useful change occur in exactly the right way for you.

7. Notice that change and the new information you've gained.

8. Re-rate and notice the difference.

NLP MODELING

Purpose: To replicate human excellence.

Author: Richard Bandler and **John Grinder**

Background: When you use your mind and body in the same way a peak performer does, you can increase the quality of your actions and thus your results. With NLP, you can imitate the success of others and improve your performance in doing so. To create NLP, Bandler and Grinder started by analyzing in detail and then went searching for what made successful psychotherapists different from their peers. The patterns discovered were developed over time and adapted for general communication and effecting change

Steps:

1. Select someone whose success you would like to imitate. Imagine yourself in her/his reality and observe her/him doing what she/he does. Focus on what she does, how she does it, why she does it and how she feels doing it.

2. Rate your level of confidence in this situation on a scale ranging from 1 (no confidence) to 10 (highly confident).

3. Refine this by learning (from this information) what is needed and not needed for success, while understanding it at a deeper level.

4. Imagine and come up with a way to teach this to others.

5. Master their beliefs, physiology, and the specific thought processes of your model. If possible, discover this information by asking them why they do what you do. Now ask yourself what does that mean to you, what if you don't do it, what is that like, what is it similar to, what about this empowers you?

6. Then, step into a full visualization (*Appendix B*) of yourself doing this, add the sights, sounds, feel, taste, and smell of doing this, modeling this person.

7. Physically perform what you are learning through modeling someone.

8. Re-rate and notice the difference.

KINESTHETIC SWISH

Purpose: To change feelings and emotions.

Author: Michael Hall and **Debra Lederer**

Background: You can use it to change a negative, self-destructive feeling into a positive, motivating feeling. You create images and sounds that lead to a certain feeling. Feelings are the core of everything. Though slower than some other swish patterns, this is still effective in changing states.

Steps:

1. Choose an unwanted feeling by remembering an upsetting feeling from your past or thinking of an upsetting feeling associated with your future or recalling an upsetting experience and letting that experience become a feeling you can locate in or on your body.

2. Rate this unwanted feeling on a scale ranging from 1 (not upsetting) to 10 (extremely upsetting).

3. Identify the upsetting feeling on or within your body. This feeling should be a sensation, not an emotion. Clear your mind.

4. In front of you, physically create your "Desired Feeling" within or on an image of a future "imaginary you" - a you who has already solved that issue. This "imaginary you" feels confident, resourceful, and has a sense of humor.

5. Put that future "imaginary you" on the floor in front of you. Clear your mind.

6. Think about the unwanted feeling and allow that feeling to rapidly diminish as it moves down your body into the ground.

7. Simultaneously, sense the future "imaginary you" with the Desired State Feeling spring up from the ground in front of you as you feel the confidence, resourcefulness, and humor coming from within the "imaginary you."

8. Step forward into the "imaginary you," and become that future "imaginary you," integrating the new resources.

9. Slowly repeat 3-5 times. Then, 3 times fast.

10. Test: Try to get another upsetting feeling. If there are no upsetting feelings, the process is complete. If you can still get the upsetting feelings, ask for the positive intention of the upsetting feelings, reframing, and repeat.

11. Re-rate and notice the difference.

COLLAPSING ANCHORS

Purpose: To get rid of negative feelings or emotions.

Author: Richard Bandler and John Grinder

Background: Collapsing Anchors can be an extremely efficient way of dealing with negative emotions surrounding historical events. Its effectiveness is hidden in the simplicity of the technique and allows even the novice practitioner an easy way of introducing personal change. Use with highly charged memories or situations as it allows for the greatest impact which itself can lead to further changes by the client. This pattern doesn't "remove" a negative emotion, but it creates a new emotion from the combination of a negative and a positive state. Often this is enough to allow the client to reprocess any traumatic event on their own.

Steps:

1. Identify negative, a situation, memory or event. See, sense, imagine, and feel this state.

2. Rate your negative feelings in this situation on a scale ranging from 1 (no pain to 10 (painful).

3. Imagine putting that negative event/situation in your non-dominant hand and making a fist. Clear your mind.

4. Release your fist and break out of the negative emotional state.

5. Identify positive state. Elicit an extreme positive state that you want instead. See, sense, and imagine everything about this positive state.

6. Put this positive state into your dominant hand and making a fist. Clear your mind.

7. Clear the positive image and relax.

8. Make fists with both hands out in front.

9. Release and open the negative, non-dominant hand.

10. Repeat and Re-rate and notice the difference.

HAVENING FOR SELF-IMAGE:
(Weight Loss & Self-Image)

Purpose: To improve self-image.

Author: *Stephen J Ruden and Ronald A Ruden* – Havening Technique

Steps:

1. Close your eyes and think of the unhelpful self-image you currently hold.

2. Rate your self-image on a scale ranging from 1 (low) to 10 (high).

3. Now, open your eyes and clear your mind.

4. Without moving your head look up, then down to the right, then down to the left.

5. Again, without moving the head, turn your eyes in a full circle, either clockwise or counter-clockwise. As soon as you have completed the circle, move them full circle in the opposite direction.

6. Place your right hand on your left shoulder and your left hand on your right shoulder.

7. Start brushing your arms downwards with your hands. Close your eyes. Imagine yourself walking along a beach and count the steps out loud from 1-20.

8. When you reach 20, sing the first few bars of any song or nursery rhyme. Stop. Open your eyes.

9. Again, without moving your head, look up then to the right, then to the left; then to the right and then to the left. Repeat five times in each direction.

10. Cross your arms as before with your hands on each opposite shoulder. Start brushing your arms again. Close your eyes.

11. Take a deep breath and slowly breathe out. When you have completely breathed out and brushed your arms at least five times, Stop. Relax.

12. Re-rate. You should be feeling much better about yourself.

To improve it still further, repeat the exercise.

1. Now, think of someone whose body you admire and imagine them standing in front of you. See how they are standing. Observe their demeanor in every respect.

2. Now, take a step forward and step into the imaginary body of that person, and, as you do so, make sure you adopt their posture and mannerisms. Feel every bit as good as you imagine they feel.

3. Step back out of that body and think of somebody who loves you.

4. Imagine that person is standing there looking at you. Mentally move into the body of the one who loves you and see yourself through their eyes and feel as they would feel.

5. Step out of that body and back into your own. Look again in the mirror but only directly into your eyes and tell yourself that you are perfect as you are and keep saying that to yourself.

21:
HYPNOKINESTHETICS
TRAINING & CERTIFICATION

Become a HypnoKinesthetics change leader and facilitator, and discover this comprehensive and empowering system you can use immediately to help yourself and others.

This HypnoKinesthetics training program was designed for coaches, hypnotherapists, psychotherapists, teachers, medical personnel and others who help people heal, change, and grow.

Do you want to become proficient in using the HypnoKinesthetics system? How good would it feel to be able to lead others through life-changing experiences? What would it be like to truly help others and witness them realizing their goals, stepping into their power, and discovering their inner joy?

These transformational tools will help you do this and more? Study with us and learn how to support others as they transform limiting beliefs and behaviors into confidence and success.

We will give you the tools you need as you coach people to make changes in habits, thoughts, feelings, and performance.

Attend our training and certification workshops to learn the most effective way to use these techniques.

You will learn to artfully use coaching skills as you guide others through the steps without interjecting solutions, interpretations, conclusions, or judgments. And you will benefit from our hands-on, one-to-one, or group training with feedback and practice sessions. We will make sure you feel confident.

HypnoKinesthetics is a therapeutic, personal empowerment system with a growing catalog of techniques and services. They will help you experience powerful change work and deep healing while gaining access to unconscious resources and solutions to life's challenges.

These groundbreaking techniques are backed up by science and research. They will allow you to help yourself and others locate, heal, and release unhealthy cellular memories.

We teach our continuing education courses in an engaging, hands-on environment. They are designed to help you master the HypnoKinesthetics system and offer life-changing care to yourself and your clients and students.

With our *HypnoKinesthetics* Certificate, you'll gain the necessary tools to become a trusted resource ready to facilitate healing, change, and growth in others.

What You'll Learn:

- The key steps, terminology, methodology, and coaching language through application exercises, case studies, and interactive program modules

- How to assess and define needed change, engage in change efforts, identify an appropriate change technique and design a strategic change plan that increases healing, change, growth and confidence building

- Help to raise awareness, build commitment, and ensure understanding, while managing outcomes as they occur

- Coaching skills and how to help clients clarify desired outcomes, establish expectations and identify realistic action steps

What's Covered in our Training:

- Coaching Skills
- Basic NLP
- Hypnosis
- Problem clarification
- Strategies for change
- Implementing HK Technique (s)
- Coaching others through kinesthetic movement
- Follow up and evaluation
- Next Steps

Who Should Take this Training?

This training is designed for use by individuals and those in helping professions including health and wellness professionals and others.

- Teachers
- Nurses
- School Counselors
- Hypnotherapists
- Life Coaches
- Psychotherapists, psychologists, counselors
- Acupuncturists
- Chiropractors
- Massage therapists
- Somatic practitioners
- Dietitians-Nutritionists
- Health Coaches
- Personal Fitness Trainers
- Trainers, workshop presenters

This training will have value for those of you who feel seasoned in your professions. It will be valuable for those of you who are new in your career. And it will be beneficial as well as for those who've had previous training. I'm happy to talk with you about your work, your challenges, and discuss how you might integrate the HypnoKinesthetics system into your work.

- Are you looking for a HypnoKinesthetics workshop or short course for your colleagues, team or members?

- Perhaps you're looking for a fresh approach to staff training, team building, and development?

- Do you want a workshop that is full of ideas and techniques that can be used immediately with real results?

- Do you want an inspirational, fun, and practical workshop or course taught by a trainer who is passionate about your results?

What We Offer:

We offer HypnoKinesthetics training workshops, coaching, consultation, and mentoring that is tailored specifically to addresses your challenges or objectives and creates a solution that meets your requirements.

Depending on your budget and what time you have available, we can adapt our workshops to be anywhere between 60 minutes to 2 days in length. The length of the course directly relates to the amount of value, knowledge, and tools we have time to share and teach.

What are the Delivery Options?

We can deliver workshops or short courses at your location, ours, at another venue site or conferences. You can select a HypnoKinesthetics workshop (which can be run once or several times) if needed, or you can request any of our other training.

Our goal is to be as flexible as possible and support you in the delivery of HypnoKinesthetics workshops that will work for you and your organization.

Contact us to talk about scheduling your training.

Let us know if you want to increase your expertise and ease in using the *HypnoKinesthetics* System by contacting us at

integritycoachingandtraining.com, calling or texting us at **206-459-2898** or emailing at **patricia@integritycoachingandtraining.com.**

CONCLUSION

"Avoiding your triggers isn't healing. Healing happens when you're triggered and you're able to move through the pain, the pattern, and the story and walk your way to a different ending."
- Vienna Pharaon

Imagine a world where everyone, young and old, has learned to manage their behavior from within themselves. Where people have discovered their inner strength, confidence, and compassion, and use them to regulate their emotions, improve their thoughts and actions, and achieve their goals. Imagine a world where people truly thrive in their lives. What would it be like if people had the tools to neutralize negative feelings from past traumatic events, move forward, and freely share their gifts, skills, and abilities with the world? How much better will our relationships be when people have coping skills and the ability to resolve current stressors and struggles quicker and more permanently? How much healthier would we be as a country if we were better able and equipped to cope with the uncertainties in an often-turbulent world?

What you have here is a recipe to support this vision. You've learned that the HypnoKinesthetics system has at its foundation, science, and research in cellular memory theory. Which states, all our experiences, including traumas, tragedies, and even triumphs and their associated emotions are stored in cellular tissues in various locations in our body. With HypnoKinesthetics, you've learned how to heal and change those memories by accessing them through movement, NLP, coaching, and hypnosis. You've also learned how to draw out, magnify, and use positive cellular memories (inner resources) to build confidence, resilience, motivation, and other inner strengths when needed.

I hope you were intrigued by the science in this book. And I hope the HypnoKinesthetics techniques helped you experience powerful change, positive transformation and deep healing as you discovered your unconscious resources and solutions to the challenges in your life.

Together we can use systems like HypnoKinesthetics to help ourselves, and others make those positive changes. So we can not only heal and grow but also gift ourselves with compassion, caring, and confidence to support others on their journey, thus bringing us all one step closer to helping, healing, and restoring our precious planet.

THE END!

Congratulations!

You've reached the end of this book. Thank you for reading! Please remember to share what you've learned here with others. When you help others succeed, you help all of us.

The information in this book is intended to augment and support all efforts to bring you and those you help, the relief you're seeking.

When choosing a practitioner to work with, always check credentials, specialized training, length of time as a practitioner, testimonials, and always trust your intuition (or gut) when making your selection.

Let this book be a helpful resource and guide to support, encourage, and help you help yourself and others make positive changes in your life starting today!

All the best!

Patricia

Connect with Patricia at:

patricia@integritycoachingandtraining.com

www.integritycoachingandtraining.com

(206-459-2898

ABOUT THE AUTHOR

*The truest expression of a people is in its dance and in its music.
Bodies never lie. - Agnes de Mille*

PATRICIA ESLAVA VESSEY

Patricia Eslava Vessey, BA, PCC, CHT, is a PCC credentialed coach through the International Coach Federation (ICF) and certified mentor coach, clinical hypnotherapist, master practitioner of NLP, certified fitness trainer, health coach, and author. She's hypnotized thousands of people in her group hypnosis classes. And she's created and presented a wide variety of personal development workshops at local colleges, conferences, and corporate events. She has also created and taught a wide assortment of fitness-exercise classes, including yoga for three decades.

Patricia created Integrity Coaching & Training Systems, a personal development company, in 2004, after 30 years doing social work in a government agency. She helps people of all ages, backgrounds, and professions heal, change, and grow by teaching them how to transform their thoughts, feelings, and behaviors. She works with individuals and groups all over the world.

As a fitness trainer and coach since 1980, Patricia has helped her students and clients to dream bigger, make better choices, and achieve powerful and lasting changes for over three decades. Attendees describe her classes as "inspiring, motivating, amazing, and life-changing." Patricia is passionate about helping people abolish limiting, negative, and destructive beliefs and behaviors so they can lead confident, successful, and fulfilled lives. Whether the transformation is in one of her fitness, wellness, leadership, or other classes, in a Hypno-coaching relationship or a conversation, Patricia's devotion to supporting others is transforming.

She loves spending time planting flowers, traveling, dancing, golfing and hanging out with her Papillion, Cooper and husband. You can learn more about Patricia and her company at IntegrityCoachingandTraining.com.

She's passionate about helping others discover, access, and thrive in their unique inner resources so they can achieve their goals and live their best life.

A:
THE POWER OF YOUR CHAKRAS

"When you touch the celestial in your heart, you will realize that the beauty of your soul is so pure, so vast and so devastating that you have no option but to merge with it. You have no option but to feel the rhythm of the universe in the rhythm of your heart.'
— *Amit Ray*

What are Chakras?

The word chakra is a Sanskrit word meaning a wheel. Chakras are subtle energy centers in the body resembling whirling wheels. With subtle similarities to meridian points in the ancient

Chinese healing art of acupuncture, the chakra energy system has its roots in East Indian healing. Chakras are much bigger acupuncture points that run along the midline of the body and contain the same energy that flows in the acupuncture meridian points. Ancient Hindus formulated that each of these energy points is connected to a different endocrine gland and body organ and has a different color. Also, each chakra spins in a clockwise direction with a different frequency.

Chakras constantly respond to our daily experiences receiving and transmitting energy from other people and the environment, thus influencing us emotionally and physically. When the chakras are clear, healed, and balanced, they are our resources for engaging with ourselves and life in the most healthy and positive ways. Therefore, we strive to achieve a healthy, healed, and balanced chakra system.

When a chakra is out of balance, we are negatively affected as is the corresponding endocrine gland and body organ associated with that specific chakra.

www.integritycoachingandtraining.com - 145 -

How many Chakra's are there?

The 7 main chakras affecting your emotional well-being are:

1. Root Chakra (red) is located at the base of the spine. The root chakra is related to safety and security, a sense of belonging and feeling supported. If we are storing weight around our belly there may be emotional issues related to security and belonging. When our root chakra is healed, balanced and functioning properly we are motivated to eat healthy and take care of our bodies.

2. Sacral Chakra (orange) is located below the navel. This chakra relates to relationships, emotional balance and sexuality. If we are overly emotional or depressed or there has been sexual abuse it may mean our sacral chakra is out of balance. This can manifest in addictions, cravings and overeating. When our sacral chakra is healed and balanced it helps us with overcoming cravings to food, drugs, cigarettes, etc.

3. Solar Plexus (yellow) is located above the navel and below the rib cage. This chakra is relating to our personal power and strength. It also governs our pancreas and blood sugar regulation which is important in weight management. When we are stressed emotionally, we will over-produce insulin which is stored as fat. When out of balance it can cause fear or lack of control. When this chakra is healed and balanced it helps us in taking our power back and in motivation to take charge over our health and eating habits. Imbalances in this chakra can also lead to eating disorders, food allergies or addictions, digestion problems and weight problems.

4. Heart Chakra (green) is located in the heart center. It is related to giving and receiving love, forgiveness and compassion towards all things including ourselves. Forgiving self and others is an important step toward healing our emotions, our bodies and our lives. The heart chakra is related to the thymus gland which impacts immune system and our adrenal glands. When out of balance we are not centered in love towards self and can use food in a self-nurturing manner.

5. Throat Chakra (blue) is located at the throat. This chakra relates to our communication, connection, speaking our truth, helping us to be heard and understood, and asking for what we need. If unbalanced, this can cause stress in the thyroid gland which is connected to our metabolism which in turn relates to how fast or slow we burn fat.

6. Third Eye chakra (indigo) is located in the center of our forehead just above and between our two physical eyes. This energy center is our chakra of wisdom and intuition. It is important in learning to trust ourselves and listen to our body's needs. When we are connected to our higher self, we are more tuned in to our needs including health and well-being.

7. Crown Chakra (violet) is located at the top or crown of our head. This chakra is related to thought, knowledge, consciousness and it is the source of our spiritual connection. When balanced and healed, this chakra helps us to also feel connected to our higher selves, spirituality and life force energies.

How do Chakras compare to Maslow's Hierarchy of Needs?

Abraham Maslow's Theory of motivation is one of the most widely discussed theories of motivation and essentially states that humans have wants and desires which influence behavior. Only unsatisfied needs influence behavior, satisfied needs don't. Since your needs are many, they're arranged in order of importance, from the basic to the complex.

As you advance to the next level of needs only after the lower level needs are at least minimally satisfied.

The further you progress up the hierarchy, the more individuality, humanness, and psychological health you will show.

Maslow's needs or motivations, from lowest to highest, are Hunger, Thirst, and Sleep; Safety, Security, Shelter, and Health; Belongingness, Love, and Friendship; Self-esteem, Recognition, and Achievement; and finally, Self-actualization.

Notice the similarities with the seven Chakras.

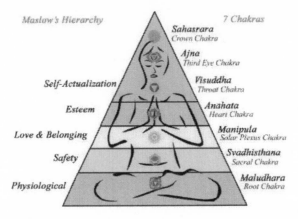

B:
AFFIRMATIONS & VISUALIZATION

"Success is a process, a quality of mind and way of being,
an outgoing affirmation of life."
- Alex Noble

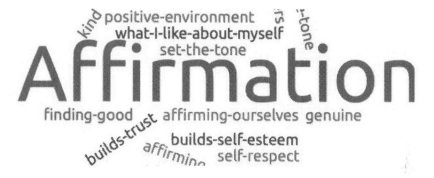

What's an Affirmation?

French psychologist **Emile Coué** first popularized self-affirmations back in the 1920s. Positive self-affirmations are statements we declare about, and to ourselves, to create a state of mind, feeling or behavior. When used effectively they can help us, for example, feel and become confident, relaxed, happy, motivated or other emotion we want to explore more often.

To truly see, you must first sincerely believe it exists.

Where Can They Be Helpful?

People use affirmations to help them make more money, manage their weight, improve confidence, performance, public speaking and more.

Used in combination with other techniques and perhaps, working with professional, positive affirmations can help you release unwanted thoughts, feelings, and behaviors while replacing them with empowering ones.

Affirmations can have a calming and refocusing effect. They also have the ability, through repetition, to permanently rewire our brain by building new, neural pathways to the thoughts, feelings, and actions we want.

Additional research on self-affirmations suggests that they can have a less than positive effect on us "if those affirmations are not part of a comprehensive program of self-growth, preferably with a knowledgeable professional;"

How to Use Affirmations:

- To use them effectively, write affirmations wisely.

- Create them in the present tense.

- Keep them short and powerful – be concise (I deserve to be confident and happy)

- Make them positive. Avoid saying what you don't want. Exclude words that indicate what you are trying to get away from or release.

- Make them realistic and believable. You know you can achieve them when you have the inner resources.

- Handwrite them, 10-20 times daily

- Visualize yourself embodying the affirmation as if it is true and happening now by adding sensory information like sights, sounds, feelings, and even tastes and smells if available.

- Repeat them daily. Use them in combination with the other tools.

- Write on stickies and place in prominent places such as mirrors, computer screens, refrigerators so that you can read them during the day.

- Say the affirmation out loud and let yourself feel it as if it's true. See, sense and imagine yourself embodying the meaning of the affirmation. Repeat for about five minutes three times a day – morning, noon and night.

- Sing your affirmation. Walk, run or dance while repeating your statement.

- If possible, look in the mirror and place your hand over your heart as you state your affirmation. Breath in, anchoring the affirmation in your body as you say it. You can even stand, sit and or gesture in a way that expresses your affirmation. Adding this movement will make it even more powerful.

- Incorporate affirmations with your daily routine such as while getting ready in the morning, lunch or afternoon break and before going to sleep and it will be easier to be consistent.

Sample Affirmations:

Adopt any of the following affirmations or create your own positive self-statements using criteria listed.

- I am learning to love and value myself.

- I deserve to be happy.

- I take excellent care of my mind and body.

- Each day I am more confident in every area of my life.

- I am good enough, and I am learning to trust myself.

Using affirmations can be a powerful step towards helping you to change your state of mind, your mood, and manifest the change you desire in your life. They work even better if you can first identify the unhelpful, counter belief that is opposing them. Once identified, additional techniques, such as EFT, hypnosis, NLP or working with a professional can help to diminish and eliminate those beliefs and behaviors.

What's Visualization?

"Make every thought, every fact, that comes into your mind pay you a profit. Make it work and produce for you. Think of things not as they are but as they might be. Don't merely dream - but create!"
- Robert Collier

Visualization is recreating all the sights, sounds, images, feelings and even tastes and smells if available relating to an activity to practice and perfect it.

According to scientists, when we use visualization, we stimulate the same regions in our brain, our motor cortex located in the frontal lobe of our minds, responsible for performing voluntary moves, just like we do when we actually perform that same action. Our thoughts produce identical mental commands as actions. This means we can use our thoughts and visualization to help us, improve our health, performance, achieve our goals and heal our body. So, when we visualize and imagine ourselves slam dunking a basketball, our brain thinks we are actually doing it.

Using the power of visualization can create miracles. For example, the actor **Jim Carrey** used visualization for years before he was successful. In 1987 he wrote a check to himself for 10 million dollars, for "acting services," and dated it Thanksgiving, 1995. Then in 1994 Jim received a check for $10 million for his role in *Dumb and Dumber.*

"I am a big believer in visualization I run through my races mentally so that I feel even more prepared."
- Allyson Felix

There are countless other examples and studies of people using visualization to overcome obstacles and create great success. For instance, **Natan Sharansky**, imprisoned in the USSR 9 years for spying for the US, regularly visualized playing chess with himself so he could improve and become a chess champ. After his release, he went on to beat the world champion chess player, **Garry Kasparov** in 1996.

Athletes and performers alike use visualization to rehearse anticipated thoughts, feelings and actions while preparing their brain and body to move and perform more effectively and to eliminate obstacles. Some of these athletes and performers who have used the power of their mind including hypnosis to enhance performance include, **Tiger Woods, Jack Nicklaus Muhammad Ali, singer, Adele, Princess Diana, Mel Gibson, Jessica Alba, Kate Middleton, Bruce Willis, Kevin Costner, Sean Connery, John Travolta, Tony Curtis, Sean Penn, Samuel L. Jackson and Robert De Niro** to name a few.

Visualization is not just for athletes, visualizing your goals, with repetition as a critical component to train and program your brain for achieving them. Simple visualization techniques help your brain to know what to look for, and they help align your actions with those goals that have become very real and achievable in your mind.

We are better prepared and more successful when we use visualization according to studies. Moreover, when we add movement and physical practice or actions to the visualizations, we improve our chances of success significantly.

Using visualization has also been shown to improve memory, enhance motivation, improve self-esteem, perception, attention span, and ability to plan and execute actions. As a fitness instructor for over 30 years, I rely heavily on visualization and mental training techniques to create, memorize, learn, rehearse and retain a significant amount of information for the various fitness classes I teach.

How does visualization work?

Begin by creating a picture or vision of yourself achieving your goal or as you would like. Be realistic and as close to reality as necessary for it to be possible. For example, I'm 5 feet tall, and it would be unrealistic for me to visualize myself as 5' 10. Avoid negative thoughts to enter your mind. Just push those thoughts aside gently and know that if you can see it mentally, you can create it in your physical reality.

See, sense, and imagine yourself in this picture adding sights, sounds, and other senses. Spend time creating the details in this image, knowing you can add even more at another time. Engage as many of your five senses as you can in your visualization. Notice your surroundings, time of day, inside, outside, objects, everything the eye can see. Notice if you are alone or with someone. Notice how you are feeling, what the feelings are and where you feel them in your body. Be aware if there is any smell in the air and what sounds you hear including what you are saying to yourself. You can add an affirmation to make this even stronger. Add even more details such as how you are standing, what you are wearing, what you are thinking and saying to yourself, and how you are feeling.

Repetition is critical, so commit to engage in this visualization at least once a daily. The best time to practice is at night or in the morning (just before/after sleep). Also, begin to turn off negative self-talk and turn on the switch for positive confidence affirming statements and affirmations. Begin praising and encouraging yourself as you would someone you love like a child or your best friend for example.

Have patience and stick with it even if it's challenging or you have doubts. With time, practice and consistency you can achieve your outcomes and create a healthy and supportive inner life leading to a new reality and self-truth for yourself that will impact your entire life.

Additional tips:

1. See yourself making progress. Feel yourself making progress and tell yourself you are becoming more and more confident every day. Imagine yourself on a movie screen in future situations with confidence and self-esteem. Watch this movie of you confidently living your life.

2. Notice how you are behaving with better self-esteem. See yourself feeling confident. See yourself successful at work, enjoying closer and more satisfying relationships, and accepting new challenges and succeeding.

3. See yourself with body language that portrays assertiveness and high self-esteem, with good posture, listening skills, and being comfortable talking to people and smiling.

4. Start recognizing more positive qualities about yourself that you like, instead of wondering if others like you. Focus on loving yourself more, and you may notice that others will also like you.

5. Realize that you are good enough right now, and you are getting better at achieving your goals.

6. Remember that self-esteem is something you used to have and you are recapturing it.

7. Combine visualization with affirmations. Say your statement during and at the end of each visualization scene. Doing this strengthens your sensory experience with a verbal message straight to your unconscious.

C:
COACHING CORE COMPETENCIES

"A good coach will evaluate your performance against your potential.
A coach helps you measure your performance against your strengths
instead of against someone else's. A coach will know what you
are capable of and will push you to your limit."
- Andy Stanley

IntegrityCoachingAndTraining.Com

International Coach Federation (ICF): What is Coaching?

Coaching is partnering with clients in a thought-provoking
and creative process that inspires them to maximize
their personal and professional potential.

A professionally trained coach provides an ongoing partnership designed to help clients produce the fulfilling results in their personal and professional lives they desire. Coaches help people improve their performances and enhance the quality of their lives.

As a professionally trained coach, you are taught to listen, to observe and to customize your approach to your individual client needs.

You seek to obtain solutions and strategies from your client; you believe the client is naturally creative and resourceful and they have the answers. The coach's job is to provide the necessary support to enhance the skills, resources, and creativity that the client already has.

Coaching Core Competencies:

The following eleven core coaching competencies were developed and designed by the ICF, to support a greater understanding about the skills and methods used within today's coaching profession. They will also support you in calibrating the level of alignment between the coach-specific training expected and the training you have experienced.

These core competencies are were instrumental designing criteria for the ICF Credentialing process examination. They are arranged into four sections based on those logically fitting together and based on common methods of viewing the competencies in each group. The groupings are not organized in any kind of priority, nor are they weighted. They are all core competencies and critical for any competent coach to demonstrate.

A. Setting the Foundation

1. Meeting ethical guidelines and professional standards
2. Establishing the coaching agreement

B. Co-creating the Relationship

1. Establishing trust and intimacy with the client
2. Coaching presence

C. Communicating Effectively

1. Active listening
2. Powerful questioning
3. Direct communication

D. Facilitating Learning and Results

1. Creating awareness
2. Designing actions
3. Planning and goal setting
4. Managing progress and accountability

For additional information on coaching visit: https://coachfederation.org/

Music Titles:

Adding music with some of the movements and techniques in this book can enhance the user's experience change work, sometimes creating a profound transformation. There are thousands of styles and types of music appropriate to use with these techniques.

Participants often ask for the title and author of the music I use in my classes. So, here is a list. I use slower, emotional songs. Please be mindful of copyrights and Fair Use Laws. Read more here: https://www.nolo.com/legal-encyclopedia/permission-sampled-music-sample-clearance-30165.html and https://info.legalzoom.com/can-use-copyrighted-song-event-22616.html

You can also find free music here: https://freemusicarchive.org/

Song and Artist:

- The Quality of Mercy - The Piano Guys

- Beethoven's 5 Secrets - The Piano Guys

- Healing - Daveed

- Coucher de Lune - Deuter

- Benediction - Jami Sieber

- Circles - Parijat - Spa Lounge

- Desert Dream Green - Deuter

- (Robot Koch Remix) - Max Richter & Robot Koch

- A Thousand Years   - The Piano Guy

- Chinese Twilight - Klaus Schonning

OTHER BOOKS

THESE BOOKS WILL TEACH YOU HOW TO HEAL, GROW, AND CHANGE & ARE AVAILABLE FROM AMAZON.

If you liked this book, you'll really like the others in our collection.

Meditation Guide For All Ages: Tips, Tools, and Techniques To Get Started (Kindle Edition)

Strategies For Mindful Living Series: Easy Actions You Can Begin Now! (Kindle Edition)

Three Ways To Program Your Mind To Lose Weight (Kindle Edition)

NOTES

- The Effects Of Negative Emotions On Our Health https://www.collective-evolution.com/2014/04/11/the-effects-of-negative-emotions-on-our-health/

- Molecules Of Emotion: The Science Behind Mind-Body https://beforeitsnews.com/power-elite/2012/10/molecules-of-emotion-the-science-behind-mind-body-medicine-2440192.html

- Bruce Lipton https://www.brucelipton.com/resource/article/the-wisdom-your-cells

- Joe Dispenza - amazon.com. https://www.amazon.com/Joe-Dispenza/e/B001IGX24Q%3Fref=dbs_a_mng_rwt_scns_share

- Is the brain the only place that stores our memories...? https://sites.bu.edu/ombs/2014/11/11/is-the-brain-the-only-place-that-stores-our-memories/

- Making Cellular Memories (https://wyss.harvard.edu/staticfiles/newsletter/newsletter-feb2010/BurrillandSilver.pdf)

- Inherited Memory in Organ Transplant Recipients (https://hubpages.com/health/Cellular-Memories-in-Organ-Transplant-Recipients)

- Inherited Memory in Organ Transplant Recipients (https://hubpages.com/health/Cellular-Memories-in-Organ-Transplant-Recipients)

- Candace Pert https://www.equilibrium-e3.com/images/PDF/The%20Research%20of%20Candace%20Pert.pdf

- https://www.consciouslifestylemag.com/cellular-memory-healing-clearing/

- http://candacepert.com/articles/where-do-you-store-your-emotions/

- A Change of Heart: Memoir-Claire Sylvia (https://www.amazon.com/Change-Heart-Memoir-Claire-Sylvia/dp/B000F6Z93W/ref=pd_bbs_3?ie=UTF8&s=books&qid=1202409655&sr=8-3)

- Feeling Emotions https://www.scientificamerican.com/article/feeling-our-emotions/

- Stress: http://time.com/4253107/americans-are-getting-more-stressed-out-study-finds/

- http://www.stress.org/americas.htm

- http://www.naturalwellnesscare.com/stress-statistics.html"%C2%A0

- Stress: https://www.psychologytoday.com/us/blog/urban-survival/201505/5-ways-stress-hurts-your-body-and-what-do-about-it

- Movement Research in Psychotherapy: *https://www.ncbi.nlm.nih.gov/pmc/articles/PMC5033979/*(Duclos and Laird, 2001; Carney et al., 2010; Shafir et al., 2013, 2016; Koch, 2014; Koch et al., 2014).

- Kinesthetic Awareness: - MASSAGE Magazine. https://www.massagemag.com/archives/Magazine/2007/issue136/Your-Body-Knows-Kinesthetic-Awareness.php

- Dance therapy: https://en.wikipedia.org/wiki/Dance_therapy

- Music Therapy: http://www.sfpinteractive.com/your-brain-on-music/

- Somatic: https://www.bridgestorecovery.com/blog/body-focused-trauma-therapy-exploring-somatic-experiencing-with-ellen-ledley/

- Kinesthesia: https://en.wiktionary.org/wiki/kinesthesia

- Kinesthetic Awareness: https://www.massagemag.com/archives/Magazine/2007/issue136/Your-Body-Knows-

- Dance Therapy Uses Movement to Address Mental Health. https://chicagohealthonline.com/dance-therapy-uses-movement-to-address-mental-health/

- Antonio Damasio – https://www.ncbi.nlm.nih.gov/pmc/articles/PMC5033979/

- https://www.technologyreview.com/s/528151/the-importance-of-feelings/

- http://www.loc.gov/loc/brain/emotion/Damasio.html

- Jean Decety Julie Grèzes https://www.researchgate.net/publication/7312997_The_power_of_simulation_Imagining_one's_own_and_other's_behavior

- 5 Ways Stress Hurts Your Body, and What to Do About It https://www.psychologytoday.com/us/blog/urban-survival/201505/5-ways-stress-hurts-your-body-and-what-do-about-it

- Learning How to Unlock Tissue Memory | IPT Patient Info https://www.iptmiami.com/news/Learning_How_to_Unlock_Tissue_Memory

- Institute of Heartmath DNA Research ARTICLE: *article* https://appreciativeinquiry.champlain.edu/educational-material/local-and-non-local-effects-of-coherent-heart-frequencies-on-conformational-changes-of-dna/

- https://www.heartmath.org/articles-of-the-heart/personal-development/you-can-change-your-dna/

- What is TimeLine Therapy? Empowerment Hypnotherapy - Leicester Hypnotherapy - FAQs. https://leicestershirehypnotherapy.com/leicester-hypnotherapy-faq-23.php; Time Line Therapy® - The Tad James Co. https://www.nlpcoaching.com/time-line-therapy/

- What is Coaching? The International Coach Federation (ICF) definition of .... http://mossperform.com/coaching-   born-or-mage/Coaching vs. Counselling | Erickson Coaching International.

- What is Somatic Syntax? https://s3.amazonaws.com/loganchristopher/nlp/Wisdom%20and%20the%20Veils%20of%20Misconception%20handout.pdf

- What is Spatial Anchoring and Sorting? http://nlpuniversitypress.com/html3/SoSto29.html, http://nlpuniversitypress.com/html3/SoSto30.html

- How to Use Affirmations: Why Self-Affirmations Don't Work - LinkedIn. https://www.linkedin.com/pulse/20140621142949-1011572-why-self-affirmations-may-not-work

- Coaching Core Competencies: ICF Competencies & Coaching Definition. https://icfwashingtonstate.com/Resources/Documents/ICF%20Competencies%20Coaching%20Definition.pdf

- Bilateral Stimulation: EMDR: The Breakthrough "Eye Movement" Therapy for Overcoming Anxiety, Stress, and Trauma (1998)

- Faster EFT: https://goe.ac/history_of_tapping.htm

- Dancing SCORE: http://www.nlpu.com/Patterns/pattern6.htm

- Energy Medicine Tool: https://www.amazon.com/Love-Code-Principle-Achieving-Happiness/dp/1101902833/ref=as_li_ss_tl?ie=UTF8&dpID=51r20W3MgoL&dpSrc=sims&preST=_AC_UL160_SR103%2C160_&psc=1&refRID=199TNKDSVZQ9Y064VTVG&linkCode=ll1&tag=theheajou06-20&linkId=6fea2957b4d4bb8dcf051bdfa52a6491

- Havening: https://www.thehavenedkind.com/what-is-havening

- Spatial Anchoring & Sorting: http://nlpuniversitypress.com/html3/SoSto30.html

- Anchoring: http://nlpuniversitypress.com/html/AaAj29.html

- Circle of Excellence: http://nlpuniversitypress.com/html/CaCom30.html

- Sad To Glad: https://www.amazon.com/NLP-Cookbook-enhancing-techniques-therapists-ebook/dp/B008CPJ0WY

- Power Stance: https://www.success-resources.com.au/blog/become-superman-just-2-minutes/

- Visual Squash: http://www.nlpu.com/Patterns/patt11.htm

- NLP Modeling: https://www.nlplifetraining.com/blog/Richard-Bandler-and-NLP-Modelling

- Kinesthetic Swish: http://steveandreas.com/Articles/kinesthetic.html

- Collapsing Anchors: http://nlpuniversitypress.com/html/CaCom46.html

- Havening Technique:
  https://www.dailymail.co.uk/sciencetech/article-3385074/How-rubbing-arms-banish-bad-memories-Havening-technique-helps-permanently-rid-distressing-thoughts.html

ONE LAST THING...

Finally, if you feel this information could help someone else, please take a few moments to let them know. If it turns out to make a difference in their life, they'll be forever grateful to you – as will I.

Let's make a difference together – one person at a time!

All the best!

Patricia

Connect with Patricia at:

patricia@integritycoachingandtraining.com

www.integritycoachingandtraining.com

(206) 459-2898

INDEX

Abraham Maslow, - 145 -

Alexander Loyd, - 121 -

Bandler, - 125 -

Bilateral stimulation, - 117 -

Collapsing Anchors, - 132 -

Dancing Score, - 120 -

Debra Lederer, - 131 -

EMDR, - 117 -

Emile Coué, - 147 -

Emotional Freedom Techniques, - 118 -

Energy Medicine Tool, - 121 -

epigenetics, - 59 -

Faster EFT, - 118 -

Fran Burgess, - 127 -

Francine Shapiro, - 117 -

Fritz Perls, - 124 -

Gary Craig, - 118 -

Grinder, - 125 -

Havening, - 123 -

International Coach Federation, - 66 -

Ivan Pavlov, - 125 -

John Grinder, - 126 -, - 130 -

Judith DeLozier, - 120 -

Max Richter, - 121 -

Michael Hall, - 131 -

Milton H Erickson, - 125 -

Paul McKenna, - 123 -

psycho-geography, - 124 -

Richard Bandler, - 129 -, - 130 -

Roger Callahan, - 118 -

Roger Sperry, - 122 -

Ronald A. Ruden, - 123 -

Score Pattern, - 120 -

Stephen J. Ruden, - 123 -

superman/woman, - 126 -

Tad James, - 64 -

The Quality of Mercy, - 121 -

TimeLine Therapy, - 64 -

Tony Robbins, - 128 -

Virginia Satir, - 124 -

Visual Squash Technique, - 129 -

Wayatt Woodsmall, - 64 -

Made in the USA
Middletown, DE
03 September 2019